LOOKING OUT THE WINDOW

Firestarter
prayers
for
your
life

David Gatward

kevin
mayhew

First published in 2002 by
KEVIN MAYHEW LTD
Buxhall, Stowmarket,
Suffolk, IP14 3BW
E-mail: info@kevinmayhewltd.com

9 8 7 6 5 4 3 2 1 0

ISBN 1 84003 936 1
Catalogue No. 1500523

Cover design by Angela Selfe
Edited and typeset by Elisabeth Bates
Printed and bound in Great Britain

Contents

For Mum and Dad

Introduction

Right, before you read on, look out of a window. Go on, push through the crowds, try not to knock anything off those shelves, get to that window (but don't go outside, you might set off the security alarm if you're still reading this book and haven't bought it yet).

What do you see? Ask yourself the question again. Anything? Look closer. Go on, really think about what you're looking at, make your mind hurt. Anything? To get you going, here are some starters:

People, children, dogs, the floor, food, drink, loneliness, laughter, the weather, thought, pain, activity, dust, age, youth, worry, stress, romance, friendship, consumerism, pressure, work, leisure, despair, fear, wonder, discovery, hope, disgust, wealth, prosperity, poverty, unemployment, faith, breakfast, dinner, tea, snacks, travel, freedom, entrapment . . .

It's a big world out there, isn't it? Huge. A miraculous blob of blue and green floating in space, spinning lives round the sun. Your life is one of them. The people outside that window are other lives. Hundreds of millions of them trying to live a life and no doubt every one of them searching for something, anything.

And so to this little book sitting in your hand. This is more than a collection of prayers (I hope). Look at it as a firestarter for your brain. Getting involved with life, getting something out of it and putting something back into it, getting out into the world . . . it isn't just about sitting around, letting your life drift on by in the hope that when you hit retirement you'll have enough of a pension to ease the thought that death isn't as far away as it used to be. If you want to get something out of life, if you want to have purpose and find out what God's ideas are on what your life's about, you've got to engage with it, get involved. You've got to think, challenge, dream, work, sweat, cry, hope, despair, keep going, run, hide, lose, win, fight . . . and through it all cling onto the hand of God no matter what. Got it? Good. Get involved.

DAVE GATWARD

PRIORITIES

Get your priorities right

James, my brother, looked at me one sunny morning and smiled a simple sentence: 'Dave, mate; you look content.' And I was. But perhaps that wasn't too difficult considering my surroundings. It was a bright Tuesday, the kind that sings when you open the door, and we were happily riding along on horseback through a river near Queenstown, New Zealand. I hadn't been on a horse for years; not since that huge dapple-grey beast decided to have a go at giving me a taste of airtime horse-style; and the experience was helping me to meet 'me' again. But how was that possible? Surely I knew who I was and what I was about? And I wasn't being unnecessarily overcome by an impromptu case of 'hippy-ness', was I? Not having only recently replaced my girly-hippy-locks with masculine short-haired-ness?

I'd arrived in New Zealand a week or so earlier; tired, stressed and wondering why the airline I'd flown with had given me a pair of free socks that were the perfect size for a child aged 10 or under. This was a trip I'd yearned for, needed and eventually saved up enough money to do, and as I stepped off the plane I was sure I heard a whisper somewhere of 'Welcome home'.

Work, I'd been told all my life, was important. I had no doubt that this was true. Without it how was I to live? You need some sense of security, a place to live, money to save and invest, a pension, a car, holidays in the south of France . . . But what I hadn't been warned about was how 'work' soon takes the place of 'life', and slowly, over time, things get distorted. For some reason I had begun to think that getting a life involved getting a sports car; and being successful, when roughly translated, meant being rich. Feeling happy involved my job and my work taking precedence over all other areas of my life. Over a number of months I had become someone who couldn't sleep, lived off caffeine, smoked, drank, and was showing a dangerous interest in investing in shares. Where was the real 'me'? What had I done with what I was really about?

At that moment in time I had very little. I was living out of the boot of a car and sleeping in a tent. None of the clothes squashed in my rucksack were fashionable. There was no television. And at long last, I was allowing myself to breathe. I thought about all the stuff I had collected around me that was sitting back in the UK waiting for me to get back. In that moment I realised how unnecessary all of it was. I had managed to fill my life with things I didn't need, and it was time to clear away some of the rubbish.

When I arrived home and walked into my flat the feeling intensified. It's amazing how the things you thought would free you, can suddenly be the things that make you feel trapped. I wanted there and then to bin everything, buy a tepee and make a living from selling small and attractive neck adornments. But that wasn't an option; getting your priorities right doesn't mean becoming a new-age traveller . . . unfortunately. It begins with the small things and, like a drop of water in a pond, the ripples soon affect the whole.

Life is all about priorities. In a world where we seem to be increasingly encouraged to sacrifice all for that dream job, wealthy lifestyle and swimming pool, it's easy to let the mind become cloudy, to lose sight of the real goal. Jesus once said, 'I came so that you may have life and live it to the full.' Next time you find things are getting a little out of balance ask yourself a simple question, 'Am I living my life to the full?' If you're not, take another look at your priorities; chances are they're not the ones you started with.

Matthew 6:25
I tell you not to worry about your life. Don't worry about having something to eat, drink, or wear. Isn't life more than food or clothing?

Luke 12:23
Life is more than food or clothing.

John 10:10
A thief comes only to rob, kill, and destroy. I came so that everyone would have life, and have it fully.

A gentle reminder

Sometimes we forget that outside our door is a world fully alive, a world buzzing and growling and sniffing and creaking and swimming and running. We need to remind ourselves that we're a part of it. Need a nice biblical reminder? Grab whatever version you enjoy reading and scan through Genesis 1 and 2. We sometimes leave these passages where we last heard them – back at Sunday school. But perhaps we can read them with a bit more understanding as to what they're about.

A wise friend of mine helped me look at this in a new way. 'Relationships,' he said, 'it's all about relationships.' And I think he's right, which will please him no end . . . Everything pretty much depends on everything else to exist, to work, to function, to have a purpose. There's a sense that everything is in some way connected, related to everything else. I'll admit I'm still trying to think these things through myself, but sometimes, when I'm out in the world, this makes sense.

It's not always easy to just get up, go out and shout, 'Hey world! We're related!' You might frighten those furry creatures in the hedgerows, or worse. Instead, just take some time out, go for a walk, take a notebook and pen and soak up the world. Why the pen and paper? Take it from me – you'll need it, though you might not know why until you're out there.

Lord,
   I'm in the middle of a field,
   on a rare sunny afternoon in April.
In the distance I can hear the occasional car,

a train zipping up the scenery
and the faint far-off hum of a jet.
The sun feels amazing, Lord.
Haven't felt that for a few months –
   my face warm and,
   when I close my eyes,
   yellow sunlight through my eyelids.

I'm out here because I needed to get away for a while,
   leave my everyday world behind
   and be reminded of what you actually created.
Why?
Don't know really.
But I'm here, pen and paper in hand,
   just in case I feel inspired or something.

Sometimes, Lord,
   I think I let my little life,
   my little self-created world,
   take over.
I replace the real picture,
   the big picture,
   with a smaller, badly-drawn version.
It's not that I'm happy with it,
   it's just that sometimes it's easier to look at.

It's a bit like TV, Lord.
Outside my door,
   (the one in my mind as well as at the front of the house)

is a world so vast,
so creative,
so alive,
that it's a bit scary.
It's often easier to deal with a reality
that's more two-dimensional.
Where people do fantastical things,
where cars blow up and no one dies,
where everyone's beautiful,
where the hero always wins.
Know what I mean?

I seem to find myself living one life
and dreaming another.
I replace the reality I'm not happy with
with the fantasy I wish was mine.
It's daft, Lord, I know,
and I guess this is me just carrying out
a reality check,
getting back to the beginning,
to what it's all about,
and where I really belong.

Lord,
in this huge world,
I sometimes feel that who and what I am
is so small, so insignificant,
that I really don't matter at all.
But standing here,
being gently reminded by your wide world

that I'm a part of it,
as much a part as these trees,
fields, birds, animals, insects,
weather changes, gusts of warm wind . . .
it helps me feel a little closer to the bigger picture,
the bigger plan.

Clear my mind, Lord.

Amen.

Genesis 1:21
So God made the giant sea monsters and all the living creatures that swim in the sea. He also made every kind of bird. God looked at what he had done, and it was good.

Genesis 1:27
So God created humans to be like himself; he made men and women.

Time out

Jesus took time out: to pray, to walk, to think, to be alone. In today's busy world we all can forget to do this. I'm not talking about being alone through no fault of your own, I'm talking about making time to be just you as you are where you are with God. But being with God doesn't necessarily mean having a heart-rending session of prayer or considering the deeper meanings behind obscure biblical passages. It can be just sitting still for a while on a park bench, reading a book, having a nap, taking a walk, listening to some music. Taking time out is about taking time to get back to who you are. Say hello to yourself again.

Lord,
   I'm shattered.
It's been a long, long day
   and I need this break.
Just a bit of 'me' time.
I'm not being selfish,
   just taking some time out.

At the moment
   life has a way of filling my mind
   with things I don't need.
From shopping lists
   to bills, projects at work,
   and lots of other stuff I can't be bothered
   to bore you with.

The point is
    that all that stuff
    pushes me out
    and I just need a bit of time
    to reintroduce myself to who I am.

I'm not sure I ever realised life would be like this, Lord.
So busy that I forget who I am,
    what I'm about.
It's odd;
    my days seem so easily to become weeks,
    months,
    until I eventually realise I've been living my life
    without actually being alive.
Instead of squeezing everything I could
    from every day
    I've just drifted through
    from one pressure to the next,
    not thinking about what's really going on
    in me.

Do you remember me, Lord?
The me that I really am?
I think I'm beginning to,
    sitting here
    away from it all.
This feels like a stolen moment,
    but it shouldn't be like that.
I need to make more time for me
    in my life.

After all, it is my life
   and you gave it to me
   to make something of.
I'm not sure caffeine and bills
   are exactly what you had in mind.

This is good, Lord.
   I can feel my brain calming a little,
   my mind relaxing,
   'me' coming back on-line.

Help me boot-up my hard drive now and again, Lord.

Amen.

Mark 1:35
Very early the next morning, Jesus got up and went to a place where he could be alone and pray.

Luke 5:16
But Jesus would often go to some place where he could be alone and pray.

Luke 6:12
About that time Jesus went off to a mountain to pray, and he spent the whole night there.

Wake-up call

I'm lucky – I don't mind mornings. I actually enjoy getting up early and getting on with the day. I have a particular dislike of lying in and letting the day drift on without me in it. One of the great joys for me is getting up at 6.30am and taking the dogs for a walk. The sun's just pushed through the horizon, cold dew clings to the grass, birds are awake and rather pleased about it. I can smell all manner of breakfasts from all over the world being cooked down our street. And the air is cold even though the day is bright and the sky clear.

OK, so it's not always like that. Sometimes I have to force myself out into the world, through the rain, only to have the dogs look at me and ask me to take them right back home again. But mornings – they're something so fantastic missed by so many because of a comfy bed and an urge to stay in the warmth rather than risk the cold.

In some respects, life is a bit like mornings. It can be all too easy to stay in bed, in the warmth and comfort of what we know, and just let the world get on with its own thing outside our own existence. There's a lot less risk that way and it's a lot more comfortable. But life isn't meant to be comfortable. Perhaps sometimes, because we're Christians, we think we should get it easy. That getting God's help means being shown an easy route, a simple way through. Bad things really shouldn't happen to us because God loves us. Not so. If I thought nothing bad should happen to me because my Dad loves me, I think he'd have a few choice words to say.

Life involves risk. It's about facing the risk of life's own cold mornings but with God by our side. If the risk was taken away where would be the sense of achievement, the sense of getting there, of doing something worthwhile, of really living, being truly alive?

If you're an early morning person you probably understand a little of what I'm on about. If you're not, you probably understand as well, just can't see that it has anything to do with getting up before the postman arrives. Either way, do yourself a favour – get up early one morning and go and breathe in the creation of a new day. Risk it. Learn from it. Go meet your God and your life early one morning. Dare you!

It's a cold one today, Lord.
Not that the dogs care,
 running around like two rather excited blurs
 of fur and slobber.
My fingertips are already beginning to tingle
 and my face stings a bit.
And it feels great!

Ten minutes ago I was still in bed.
It's a bit of a struggle to get up but always worth it,
 no matter how much my tired limbs complain.
Once out, I feel so suddenly alive
 that I think other dog-walkers avoid me
 because of the big mad grin on my face.
Not that I care – I love mornings.

I blame Dad for getting me into this whole
 early morning thing.
'Why waste the day?' he'd say,
 and off he'd go out the door at six,
 clad in wellies, wax jacket and hat,
 to chop wood or walk the dog
 or take the gun out and try to scare a few pigeons.

And now, looking back,
    I think he had a point.
'Why waste the day?'
Indeed, why waste it?
OK, so a lie-in is nice now and again,
    but to get up and head out into the break of the day
    is something I now find hard to live without.

I think mornings, Lord,
    help me remember what my life's about.
If I just lie around in comfort not willing to get up,
    risk the cold and the all too frequent rain,
    I miss out on something wonderful:
    the dawn of a new day.
Just think what I'll miss
    if I avoid the cold and the rain of my life
    just so that I can stay comfy and warm . . .

Makes sense to me anyway, Lord.

Amen.

Mark 4:19
But they start worrying about the needs of this life. They are fooled by the desire to get rich and to have all kinds of other things. So the message gets choked out, and they never produce anything.

Luke 17:33
People who try to save their lives will lose them, and those who lose their lives will save them.

I'm a dreamer

Right, I admit it. Full-on, hands-in-the-air admission – I'm a dreamer. Always have been and always will be. I'm not talking day-dreaming here, though I have been known to sit in the sun and just 'imagine' for a while. I'm talking about real dreams, about my life, what it's about, what I'll become, what my purpose is, what I'll achieve. About my friends and family, where we'll all end up, what we'll all do. Dreams of what God's about, what heaven's like, what happens when I get there. These are dreams that can and will affect my life.

Dreams can be dangerous. They can take over, take the place of real life. They can also bring freedom; a freedom to go for what you believe in, to have the drive and faith to not let go.

Life can erase our dreams all too easily. Before we know it we've forgotten what we really honestly dreamed of doing with our lives and instead we're just living. We find ourselves thinking that we have to be realistic, that we've got responsibilities now, that other things are more important. Important yes, but more important?

I can't live without my dreams. And I have a feeling that the good ones, the ones I'm really going for, are there with a little help from God. I have a sprinkling of ability, which if I put my mind to it and refuse to give up, could help me realise my dreams. But I also know that I can't achieve what I'm really capable of without God's help. Now that's my real dream – to achieve what I'm really capable of with God.

Lord,
    thinking back a few years,
    I remember thinking that by now

that big dream of mine would be a reality.
Well, in many ways, it isn't.

It'd be easy to sit here and think of lots of excuses
    or even blame you.
But that's pointless.
All I'd get out of that is nothing at all.
Know what I mean?

Thing is though, Lord,
    I can see the dream better now.
It seems more in focus.
I'm closer to it than I was years ago.
I've a long way to go, but I haven't given up.
I've stuck with it regardless,
    chosen it over other ideas,
    put it before other possibilities.

At times it's been hard.
Well, to be honest,
    most of the time it's been hard.
Holding onto a dream,
    not giving up or giving in
    can be nightmarish.

You find other people overtaking you,
    achieving their dreams before you,
    flying ahead at such a pace
    that soon you find it hard to see them.
It makes you want to pack up and go home.
But that's not very me, Lord, is it?

Seeing people achieve their dreams
only serves to make me more determined.
And this one dream, Lord,
is all wrapped up in my faith in you.
That's not to say I want you to make it easy for me,
just that I want to know you're with me.

Lord,
I've got a long way to go yet, I know,
but I know now that with every step I take,
no matter how hard,
I'm edging just that little bit closer.

Walk with me, Lord.

Amen.

Psalm 138:8
You, Lord, will always treat me with kindness. Your love never fails. You have made us what we are. Don't give up on us now!

Proverbs 19:21
We may make a lot of plans, but the Lord will do what he has decided.

Romans 8:28
We know that God is always at work for the good of everyone who loves him. They are the ones God has chosen for his purpose.

Under pressure

Pressure seems to come hand in hand with life. There's nothing you can really do to get away from it. Remember how easy life seemed when summer holidays lasted for ever and all you really wanted to do was just run and run and run? When adulthood seemed so far away that it was almost inconceivable that you'd ever be out of your teens and into your twenties and beyond?

I remember when pressure started to become a part of my everyday life. When homework turned into exams which in turn turned into having a job. Sometimes I start to resent the pressure I'm under and get depressed. Not very helpful. But I know that pressure is something I have to learn to deal with, to live with and control. And sometimes, it can actually help as it sharpens my thoughts, gives me a bit of a buzz.

Jesus wants to get involved in every bit of our lives, and that goes for the times when the pressure builds so high you think your head might just explode. Take some time out, go for a stroll, lie down, think . . . and send up a prayer no matter how brief. Every storm has an eye, just sometimes you need help to find it.

Lord,
    I feel like I'm about to burst.
I can feel tension in my finger tips
    and I keep clenching my fists.
I can't sleep,
    I can't eat,
    I can't relax.

I'm so stressed
   I don't know where to turn
   or what to do.

At times like this,
   all I want to do is lie down
   and forget about it all.
Just avoid it and hope it all goes away.
Never does, though.

The pressure I'm under is affecting all of my life.
At work, at home,
   with friends and family.
Everything is suffering
   and I don't know what to do.

It's as if everything's come to a head.
It's crazy at work,
   it's crazy at home.
There are bills to pay,
   things to sort out,
   and I'm unable to do it all.
I don't know what to do.

Lord,
   I need, for just a moment,
   a sense of peace,
   of calm.
To know that in this storm
   there is an eye

where I can rest for a moment
and watch it all spin out of control around me.
That's all I ask for, Lord.

Guide me to the eye of the storm, Lord,
   and out the other side.

Amen.

Matthew 8:23-27
After Jesus left in a boat with his disciples, a terrible storm suddenly struck the lake, and waves started splashing into their boat. Jesus was sound asleep, so the disciples went over to him and woke him up. They said, 'Lord, save us! We're going to drown!'

But Jesus replied, 'Why are you so afraid? You don't have much faith.' Then he got up and ordered the wind and the waves to calm down. And everything was calm.

The men in the boat were amazed and said, 'Who is this? Even the wind and the waves obey him.'

Worrying about tomorrow

Right, check out Matthew 6:34. There's not much I can add to this really, is there? But we all seem to ignore this simple lesson. Why worry about tomorrow when today has enough trouble of its own? How much more wisdom can we really handle? We spend so many days thinking about tomorrow, what could happen, what it's all about, what might go wrong, that often we forget the here and now. We clutter it up with thoughts about what might be rather than what is. Not only that, we convince ourselves that tomorrow is generally something that involves stuff we're not looking forward to. That's why we worry about it. Too many questions beginning with 'What if?'

Every day is a new day. Every day brings with it possibilities, new discoveries, excitement, adventure. Tomorrow will always be one step away, jam-packed with worries and situations that probably won't ever happen because most of the time we invented them. So take Jesus' lead on this. Don't worry about tomorrow, deal with today. That's where we are and that's where he meets us.

Lord,
   I'm worried about tomorrow.
I'm not just talking
   about what I'll be doing at work in a few hours' time
   but the whole of my life.

What's round the corner, Lord?
What's going to happen to my life?
I wouldn't mind a peek now and again
   because at the moment I feel a little bit afraid.

There seems to be so much to do,
   so much that could happen,
   and my life seems suddenly so short.

Do you hear this a lot, Lord?
Prayers from people scared of what tomorrow may bring?
Afraid of what could happen?
It's frightening
   because so much of life
   is unplanned,
   out of our control.

Thing is though, Lord,
   what's the point of worrying?
What good does it do me?
All that happens
   is that I get all confused,
   nervous,
   and get myself wound up.
Worrying about tomorrow doesn't solve anything.
And sometimes I do it too much.

Lord,
   I know tomorrow's scary
   but at the same time
   it's exciting.
If I really did know what was going to happen in my life
   I'd be rather disappointed.
The sense of discovery,
   of having a say in what I do,

where I go,
would all be gone.
Couldn't live like that.

Help me, Lord,
to see tomorrow as something
to look forward to,
something full of new discoveries
about my life.

Worrying about tomorrow
is a waste of today –
help me remember that.

Amen.

Matthew 6:34
*Don't worry about tomorrow. It will take care of itself. You have
enough to worry about today.*

The real me

Find something that you can see your reflection in. If you're in the house, use a mirror or a shiny oven dish. If you're outside, use a puddle, a pond, a lake, a silvery crisp packet. Look at yourself. What do you see? Just a face? If that's the case, look deeper, look beyond your eyes, and try to stare into the reflection of who you actually are. Seeing more? Is the picture getting clearer?

Seeing ourselves is sometimes very difficult. Life takes over, we let it run riot with who we are and before we know it we've lost sight of what we're about. Soon enough we're just living a life as someone else rather than as the person we know we can be. Not only that, we're all guilty of just seeing that bad side of ourselves, the dirt in our lives – what's bad, rather than good in who we are.

Now look again at that reflection of yourself and think about what God sees, what's really behind that reflection. Think of all that potential, all those dreams, all that laughter and love and hope and life. God knows we're not perfect but sees the good in us, what we're really capable of. After all, he's not interested in the righteous but the sinners. People like you and me. Real people with real problems, real pain, real potential. Now, which reflection should you dwell on? Simple answer, isn't it? God sees you, the real you. Perhaps you should take a look now and again . . .

Lord,
    can you see me?
The real me?
The me you created?

The me I actually like?
The image is a bit blurred at the moment, Lord.
Can't quite get it in focus.

It seems ages now,
   since I was last happy with who I am.
I've lost sight of who I am,
   what I'm about,
   what I'm trying to do with my life.
I feel like I'm living my life
   as someone else,
   someone I don't really like.
Does that make sense?

I think I've let life get in the way a bit.
It's taken over and pushed me out.
I'm still living
   but not as me.
Days go by
   but I don't seem to be getting much out of them.
I'm not growing,
   developing,
   learning.

I think, Lord,
   I need to take stock of where I am.
I know life is busy,
   that sometimes it can take over
   and it's all you can do
   to keep your head down,

but I need to remember who I am,
who you want me to be.

I know, Lord,
that with you
I am worthwhile,
that I have purpose,
and it's that image
that I need to see again.

Help me see myself clearly again, Lord.

Amen.

Matthew 10:30-31
Even the hairs on your head are counted. So don't be afraid! You are worth much more than many sparrows.

Matthew 9:13
'Go and learn what the Scriptures mean when they say, "Instead of offering sacrifices to me, I want you to be merciful to others." I didn't come to invite good people to be my followers, I came to invite sinners.'

Mark 2:17
Jesus heard them and answered, 'Healthy people don't need a doctor, but sick people do. I didn't come to invite good people to be my followers. I came to invite sinners.'

The bigger picture

What's your place in this world? Any idea? Is it where you are now, where you're going to, where you'll be in a few years time? Or do you find thoughts about where you are in the future of everything disappear as life fills up with appointments and meetings and deadlines and bills?

Sit back for a few minutes. Close your eyes and just breathe. Think about the world around you. Start from where you are and go for a walk in your mind. Take a look around your house and see your place in it, your life, your influence. Now venture outside, into the garden or down the road. See people you know, think of people you love, people you help, people you work with. See how your lives entwine, become a part of each other and co-exist. Now think further, think wider. Stroll around this world, these countries. Look at the people living their lives, what they're doing. You're a part of that, a part of the bigger picture.

Our lives have purpose, meaning, reason. It's up to us to live it and breathe it, to eat and sleep it, to walk with it and run with it. The bigger picture is just that – big. And perhaps the only way to ever be noticed, to ever have an impact, to ever be worth something, is to make your part of that picture vibrant and rich with the colour of your life.

Lord,
    you there?
My life's so full,
    so busy,
    that I'm finding it difficult to see anything at all,
    including you.

My mind feels stuffed with information
    it doesn't need.
Things to do,
    things to sort out,
    things to get,
    things to plan,
    things to achieve,
    things to pay for . . .
    all of this seems to be distorting my vision,
    blurring my view.

There's a bigger picture, Lord,
    and I wouldn't mind being able to see it again.
I caught a glimpse of it a while ago.
I was happy with what I was doing,
    felt that I was going somewhere,
    but recently that's all got a bit lost.
Now I'm so busy being busy
    I've lost sight of what it's all about.

Can you see me, Lord?
Or do I look blurred to you as well?
Have I become so consumed by my everyday life
    that I've drifted off from where you want me to be?
It feels like that sometimes,
    that even if I were to search
    you'd be so far away that I'd never find you.

I don't want to live like this, Lord.
I want to get back on track,

sort myself out with life,
with you.
I want to see that bigger picture again, Lord,
the picture you're helping me paint,
full of the colours of my life.
Colours I want to be vibrant,
exciting,
filling the canvas with an explosion
of everything that I am.

Show me where to paint next, Lord.

Amen.

Matthew 10:29-31
Aren't two sparrows sold for only a penny? But your Father knows when any one of them falls to the ground. Even the hairs on your head are counted. So don't be afraid! You are worth much more than many sparrows.

Genesis 1:27-30
So God created humans to be like himself; he made men and women. God gave them his blessing and said:

'Have a lot of children! Fill the earth with people and bring it under your control. Rule over the fish in the sea, the birds in the sky, and every animal on the earth. I have provided all kinds of fruit and grain for you to eat. And I have given the green plants as food for every-thing else that breathes. These will be food for animals, both wild and tame, and for birds.'

Genesis 2:4-7

That's how God created the heavens and the earth. When the Lord God made the heavens and the earth, no grass or plants were growing anywhere. God had not yet sent any rain, and there was no one to work the land. But streams came up from the ground and watered the earth. The Lord God took a handful of soil and made a man. God breathed life into the man, and the man started breathing.

Which way now?

Life is like a map. Apparently. At times it seems more like a big bowl of over-cooked spaghetti. A tangle, a mess, a confusion. We don't know which way to go, which route to follow, which path to take. The more we pray, the worse it gets, the worse it gets the worse we feel.

The trouble with life is that we always want to see where we're going, what's round the next bend. But think how dull life would be if that was the case. If we knew exactly what was going to happen next, could plan for it, deal with it and go on from there. Wouldn't be much fun left, would there?

Perhaps life is a map, but only God gets to see that. There are literally billions of routes we can take to get from one side to the other. Some are good, some are bad and maybe God knows them all. Perhaps all God wants to do is gently help us make the right decisions from wherever we are. We have the freedom to go whichever way we choose, that's the gift of life and the gift of freedom God gave us. What we need to do is remember to rejoice in that freedom and, even if we do make the wrong choice, thank God that we were in a position to make it rather than have it made for us.

Lord,
    which way do you want me to go?
I've reached another crossroad,
    another place in my life
    where a decision needs to be made,
    and I don't know what to decide.

Whichever way I go
  there's risk.
The risk of failure,
  of having gone the wrong way.
But then I'm not actually sure that either way
  is wrong
  or right.
It's not really a case of choosing the right path.
Each path seems to have its good and bad points,
  its own risks and dangers.
Yes, Lord,
  I am confused.

I've been putting off the deciding bit
  for quite a while now.
Seemed a safer way to go about it.
I knew the decision would have to be made
  but if I just avoided making it for a while
  it wouldn't seem so bad.
But now I've got no choice.
There's no time left to waste.
I've got no choice but to turn whichever way I choose
  and walk,
  no turning back.

It's scary, Lord.
This is a big moment,
  a big decision.
One I've been building up to for quite some time.
And the only way I can do this,

the only way I can be sure that whatever I choose
I have a chance of succeeding,
is by carrying this out with you.

Lord,
I think I know what to do,
which way to go.
I'm scared,
I'm uncertain,
but I'm also excited.

Walk with me, Lord,
down this new road.

Amen.

Matthew 7:13-14
Go in through the narrow gate. The gate to destruction is wide, and the road that leads there is easy to follow. A lot of people go through that gate. But the gate to life is very narrow. The road that leads there is so hard to follow that only a few people find it.

Dirty feet

Right, hands up who get bogged down most days in feeling unworthy of God's love. If your hand's not stretched high, you're lying. It's a part of life, isn't it? No matter what we do, no matter how much we try to get things right, we still feel unworthy, dirty, grubby. But then, how could we ever feel any different? We're all flawed – perhaps that's one of the reasons God finds us so interesting!

You only have to skim through the New Testament to see what Jesus was all about, what his message was. It may be basic stuff this, but sometimes I think we need to just look at our faith and get back to the basics now and again, remind ourselves what it's really about. Jesus made a point of hanging about with people who weren't the cleanest of individuals. He made fishermen and prostitutes and tax collectors his friends. He came specifically to show us where God belonged, who God loved . . . and this is the good bit, he loved people like you and me.

When you get struck by the thought that everything you do is worthless, that no matter how hard you try you'll never become what God knows and wants you to become, think back to Jesus' crowd, his friends, the people he mixed with. Now think of the people he really had a go at, the ones he made no bones about telling were not getting things right even though they thought they were. Which group do you belong in? Which group do you want to belong in?

Lord,
    I'm not perfect.
I mean, just look at me.
My life's one big grubby mess.

I believe in you,
    try to follow you,
    get to grips with your teaching,
    but I wonder if it really shows.
There seems to be so much mud in my life
    that getting even a glimpse of you
    in what and who I am
    is most times
    nigh on impossible.

Sometimes I wonder if I'm really trying
    all that hard.
Other times I know that I am –
    it's just not having the desired effect.

Am I faulty goods?
When I was created
    was something left out?
Hope not, Lord,
    but I can't help but feel
    that's the case.

I spend most days
    feeling dirty, unclean, grubby.
When I think of you I feel even worse –
    a bit like a sheet drying in the sun
    that has this massive stain on it that everyone can see.
No matter how much I get washed,
    it's still there.

But then again, Lord,
    I sit back and think how amazing it is
    that you don't expect me to be perfect.
When I read what you did all those years ago,
    about how you went out of your way
    to mix with people who knew they were unclean,
    I feel almost at home.

It's as though through those passages
    I hear you saying to me,
    'It's OK, David!
    Get with the programme!
    I'm not here for those who think they're clean
    and spend most of their lives showing off about it!
    I'm here for those who know they're dirty,
    who know that they may never be truly clean.
    That's why I came
    and that's why I love you,
    dirty feet and all!'

And then,
    in those quiet moments,
    I sense your love,
    your compassion,
    your smile when you look at me
    through all the dirt,
    all the grime,
    and still love me –
    dirty feet and all.

Amen.

Matthew 9:9-12

As Jesus was leaving, he saw a tax collector named Matthew sitting at the place for paying taxes. Jesus said to him, 'Come with me.' Matthew got up and went with him.

Later, Jesus and his disciples were having dinner at Matthew's house. Many tax collectors and other sinners were also there. Some Pharisees asked Jesus' disciples, 'Why does your teacher eat with tax collectors and other sinners?'

Jesus heard them and answered, 'Healthy people don't need a doctor, but sick people do.'

Romans 5:6-11

Christ died for us at a time when we were helpless and sinful. No one is really willing to die for an honest person, though someone might be willing to die for a truly good person. But God showed us how much he loved us by having Christ die for us even though we were sinful.

But there is more! Now that God has accepted us because Christ sacrificed his life's blood, we will also be kept safe from God's anger. Even when we were God's enemies, he made peace with us, because his Son died for us. Yet something even greater than friendship is ours. Now that we are at peace with God, we will be saved by his Son's life.

And in addition to everything else, we are happy because God sent our Lord Jesus Christ to make peace with us.

I've got a plan

Take a breather from your day. Grab a piece of paper and a pen. Now time yourself - for five minutes write down everything you have planned for your life. Loose plans, mad ideas, things you'd like to try, daft things you'd like to do, stuff you want to see, taste, experience, places you want to go, people you want to be with, things you want to learn, skills you want to develop. Be as wild and daft as you want, think big, really, really big. Think of everything you really could do if you just had that chance.

Right, now look at that piece of paper. If you need some more time, then keep writing, get those things down in black and white so that they stare you back in the face. What you now have is a challenge, a full-on gauntlet. Your life is staring at you saying, 'Well? What you going to do about it then? Come on! What's stopping you?'

Chances are that on that list in front of you is a whole bunch of stuff that if you put your mind to it you could do. And this life is your only chance to do it. A rough quote from a film I can't quite remember went something along the lines of, 'Regrets are so much more frightening than failures.' Now that's wisdom for you! That list is everything you could do if you wanted to, if you pushed yourself and went for it. Some of the things you may fail at, some you'll really make a mess of and others you'll do brilliantly. But surely it's better to have tried and failed than to have never tried at all? Stop saying 'what if'; get involved in your life, live it. Live that plan.

Lord,
    what do you want me to do with my life?
I've been looking everywhere
    for some sign of your purpose for me
    and to be honest,
    I haven't found anything,
    not a jot.

I know so many people who seem to have found
    their purpose,
    their aim,
    and all I seem to be doing
    is just drifting from one thing
    to the next
    trying to find out what's right for me.
    It's not the greatest way to live a life, Lord.

If you do have a plan for me,
    could you let me know some time,
    or at least give me a hint?
It's hard down here
    trying to live a life of purpose
    when you're not quite sure
    what that purpose is.

It's easy to say things like,
    'Oh, yes, well, my purpose
    is to make the light of Jesus shine
    through everything I do each day.'
It's easy, and also rather self-righteous
    and not very me.

Why?
Well, that's not really a purpose,
   it's just something you should be doing anyway,
   it's what it's all about, if you get my meaning.

What I'm on about, Lord,
   is what I'm here for,
   what I'm here to do,
   to achieve with this life you've given to me.
It's such a gift
   and I don't want to waste it.
I don't want, at the end of it,
   to look back
   and have nothing to show for what I've done.

There's a danger that this could sound like pride,
   but it's not.
I want my life to count for something.
I don't want it to be an existence
   that achieves nothing more
   than being alive for a while.

I have dreams, Lord,
   big dreams of what I'm capable of.
And we both know that in my heart of hearts
   these are what I'm going for.

I sometimes wonder, Lord –
   when I'm asking if you have a purpose for me,
   is it simply out of frustration?

I want my purpose to be now
 rather than tomorrow.
I don't want to have to wait for it.
But when I think about my dreams,
 what I'm really trying to do with my life,
 I can't help but wonder if that is my purpose.
To strive for my dreams,
 to never give in,
 to keep getting back up every time I get kicked down,
 and in the end,
 when it all becomes clear,
 to be able to thank you for it.

Help me stay on target, Lord.

Amen.

Exodus 9:16
But he has kept you alive, just to show you his power and to bring honour to himself everywhere in the world.

Psalm 138:8
You, Lord, will always treat me with kindness. Your love never fails. You have made us what we are. Don't give up on us now!

Proverbs 19:21
We may make a lot of plans, but the Lord will do what he has decided.

FAITH

Fireside faith

It was a cold morning. The kind where the dew sits frozen and covers the fields in short-lived diamonds. Birds were competing to give the sun the best chorus. A couple of planes were chasing destinations across the sky. And I was out walking the dog with my dad, trying to prove that I too could wake at 6am and be bright, breezy and full of the joys of life.

A cough and a splutter and a few minutes into the walk, we started to chat. About this and that and what was what. Generally chats with my dad involve at least one deep question about life or faith or both and we soon got onto something more than what we were going to cook up for breakfast when we got back.

For some reason we got onto faith. I think I was experiencing one of my many, 'What's it all really about, Dad?' moments. Life was confusing me into a big spin, I was questioning everything and getting more confused. But what was really getting to me was that even though I questioned it, ran away from it, even rejected it, I still had a faith. I needed answers. Good solid answers. Who better to turn to than my own father? The one person who's always helped me find answers, no matter what the question?

So, feet wet with dew, nose cold and hands shoved firmly into my pockets, I asked him, 'What's faith all about, Dad?'

'In what sense?' he said.

'Oh . . .,' I replied, 'I don't know really.' Now I had to think of something, come up with something worth discussing, but I couldn't. 'Why is it that I just can't get away from my faith? Why is it always there no matter how rubbish my life gets?' I was pleased with that. Pretty much summed up my feelings.

Dad though, went silent for a few moments. He whistled for the dog and we both watched the daft mutt fling itself towards us like a guided missile. As the dog arrived, Dad breathed out a sigh and said simply, 'Fireside faith, mate.' And that was it. No real answer, no in-depth discussion, just three words.

Years later those words have stuck with me. The simple truth behind them I still find amazing. Leading by example, I think my dad's managed to bring me up with not only a faith, but a freedom to question. He's always been there to listen, to chat, to discuss. And it was generally by the fireside. You see, faith to my dad is not about deep emotional prayer or heavy Bible study. Neither is it about exciting services in church or pilgrimages abroad. To him all these things have their place, but at the very heart - or hearth - of what it's all about is his belief in a Jesus you can sit down with by a fire and just chat - fireside faith. A faith in a Lord who will walk with you, talk with you, cry with you, be with you. A Lord who will happily sit down by an open fire, share a bottle of wine, and talk through life's ups and downs. A faith with the freedom to question and to still believe.

Psalm 42:8
Every day you are kind, and at night you give me a song as my prayer to you, the living Lord God.

Psalm 66:20
Let's praise God! He listened when I prayed, and he is always kind.

Doubt

The trouble with faith is that doubt plays such a major role. It's always there niggling away at us. It's a scary thing and can very easily send your brain into a spin and before you know it nothing makes sense and you wish you could just explode. Not very useful, perhaps, but you'd certainly feel better.

So, is doubt a good or a bad thing? Bit of both perhaps? We all doubt, even those shiny Christians we've all seen on stage who sweat faith and bring millions to meet with Jesus for the first time. Even Cliff Richard doubts. And Jesus on the cross screamed, 'My God, why have you forsaken me?' Perhaps not doubt in the sense we experience it, but a hint of Jesus questioning what it's all about.

Doubt scares me but also plays an important part in who and what I am and what my faith means to me. It helps me to question, to really think through what I believe, to discuss my ideas and thoughts. It helps me not to be afraid of what's in front of me, to face up to things I don't understand, to always try and find an answer. But what really amazes me about doubt is that even when I doubt, I still believe. It doesn't make sense but it's always been the case, which is probably why, when I doubt the most, I pray about it.

Lord,
   you there?
I'm experiencing one of those dreaded moments
   of doubt.
I'm sitting here
   talking to you
   and not quite believing that you're there listening.

My faith, Lord,
   seems to swing rapidly from brief moments
   of security
   to huge expanses of emptiness and insecurity.
I seem to spend most of my life
   questioning whether what I believe
   is true,
   if it's helping me get through my life,
   if I'm just an idiot,
   if I'd be better off without it.

I look at so many other people
   who haven't got one ounce of interest
   in getting to know you
   and their lives don't seem to be any worse for it.
I look at some of them
   and to be honest they seem to be much, much happier
   than I ever am.
Doesn't make sense, Lord.

I know it's all about faith,
   and that faith implies that proof's not needed,
   that I don't and shouldn't need
   to be struck down by your voice one morning
   or to have a vision of such startling clarity
   that instantly I'm a true believer.
But most of the time, Lord,
   faith isn't always enough
   and I'm desperate for proof.

Trouble is,
    I then start looking around me
    and I see proof.
I see this world
    and what it's capable of.
I see this creation
    and how amazing it is.
I look at me,
    my friends, my family,
    and I'm amazed and see you in it all.
But then I start thinking that this isn't enough,
    that more proof is required.

Do I always sound so confused, Lord?
I wonder sometimes, I really do.
Seems I only ever come to you with questions,
    problems, doubts.

I guess this will never really change.
That through my whole life
    I'll always believe
    and always doubt.
It's a battle that I'll always have to fight.

But even when I do doubt, Lord,
    even when I completely and totally
    don't believe in you,
    can't see anyway for any of it to be true,
    there's still something that keeps me in your fold.
It's a sense, Lord,

a sense of something,
of you,
of what it really is all about.
And in those moments,
    when doubt is at its greatest,
I don't doubt any more.

Amen.

Matthew 14:31
Straightaway, Jesus reached out his hand. He helped Peter up and said, 'You don't have much faith. Why do you doubt?'

John 20:27
He greeted his disciples and said to Thomas, 'Put your finger here and look at my hands! Put your hand into my side. Stop doubting and have faith!'

Prayer

Prayer really confuses me. One day I'm wondering if I do enough, next day I realise I've spent most of the day praying. Then I wonder if I'm doing it right at all, then I think, 'Well, is there actually a right way at all?' I started writing prayers simply because it helped me to focus on what I was thinking about, what I was trying to say, what I was really trying to get off my chest. And it works, for me anyway.

The thing with prayer is that perhaps the only wrong way of doing it is not to do it at all. It's not a competition to see who can do it the most or the best. God definitely isn't keeping a tally in heaven of when you pray and then marking it out of ten on content, delivery, purpose, depth. It's about communicating with your creator, getting in touch, making that connection.

I am personally terrible at setting specific times aside to pray. I just can't do it. I simply don't live my life like that (just you ask anyone who knows me). When I think about it I realise I pray pretty much all the time. How? Well, prayer to me is no more and no less than chatting to a mate. And with mates you generally chat a lot. By email, by phone, over a pint. So I find myself praying almost everywhere I am. After all, if God's everywhere and loves me, why shouldn't I?

Lord,
    I've been doing this for years
    but I still don't feel that I'm making a very good job of it.
I don't feel like I do it enough,
    practise it enough,
      try different ways of doing it enough.

Is there a right way to pray, Lord?
It feels as if I am at the start of my whole faith
   talking like this,
   but to be honest,
   in the years I've been following you
   I don't really feel that things have improved
   all that much.

What do you think, Lord?
How does it seem from your side of things?
Am I doing OK?
Or am I doing it all wrong and really getting on your nerves?
Because I'm getting on mine, that's for sure.

I'm useless at setting aside time each day
   to talk to you.
It's not that I don't take prayer seriously,
   don't take you seriously,
   it's simply something I don't do.
I've tried it,
   set time aside
   and then just forgotten about it
   or not bothered.

I'm terrible at praying about all the right things.
I get so bogged down by this that and the other
   that I forget to pray about
   other more important stuff.
It's not that I don't think about that other stuff,
   just that I find myself going off at a tangent,

getting stuck,
not knowing how to change tack
or just to focus on what I'm on about.

And, Lord,
I'm awful at sticking to praying.
I start off with all the right intentions
then moments later
my mind wanders off and I'm onto something else
and our conversation has been taken over
by the really important tasks in life
like putting the rubbish out.

I can't seem to help myself, Lord.
It seems that the only way I ever speak to you
is in snatched conversations,
stolen moments of my day.
If I'm worried,
up goes a little prayer.
If I'm happy,
I say thank you.
If I'm unsure,
I pray a little question.

Which gets me thinking . . .
OK, Lord,
so I may not prostrate myself on the ground
on a regular basis,
I may not kneel in supplication
desperate to feel moved by your Word,

but I do communicate
each and every day.
Thinking about it,
  I seem to talk to you most of the time.
That's not too bad then, is it Lord?

Amen.

Matthew 23:13-14
You Pharisees and teachers of the Law of Moses are in for trouble!
You're nothing but show-offs. You lock people out of the kingdom
of heaven. You won't go in yourselves, and you keep others from
going in.

Matthew 6:9-13
You should pray like this:

Our Father in heaven,
  help us to honour your name.
Come and set up your kingdom
  so that everyone on earth will obey you,
  as you are obeyed in heaven.
Give us our food for today.
Forgive us for doing wrong,
  as we forgive others.
Keep us from being tempted
  and protect us from evil.

God in every day

How easy is it to see God when you're having a good day? And have you noticed how this situation generally reverses if it's a bad day? If things are fine and everything's right with the world then God's great and we're happy and everything is best, best, best. If things aren't fine and everything's wrong with the world then God does not exist and we can't see the point in any of it and everything just gets worse and worse and worse. Confusing, isn't it?

The thing is, no matter what the day's like, God's there in the midst of it. This doesn't mean that we should blame God when things go wrong. What it does mean is that whether life is good or bad, on the up or plummeting down, God's with us, experiencing life as we live it and, in the same way any friend would, wants to help us through it. After all, if life's on a downward spiral our friends and family can't really do all that much to alter the situation. But what they can do is support us, be there for us, love us, live with us. That's what God does, only more so – he's looking after our souls too.

Today's been awful, Lord.
Everything's gone wrong,
   everything's been awful
   or a mistake
   or a problem.
I haven't seen you anywhere
   and it's been a little lonely.

It all started this morning
   when I stubbed my toe on the bed,

Then burnt the toast
and spilt the coffee.
Then,
    on the way to work,
    I realised I'd left something I needed at home
    and had to turn back,
      making me late.
From that point on it just got worse.
Nothing I did was right,
    everyone thought I was wrong.
Even my sandwiches were rubbish.
When I got home the house was cold,
    there was nothing in the fridge
    and I was too tired to do anything.

It's been a really rubbish day
    and I don't seem to have been able to see you
    in any of it – unless of course it was all just
    a big practical joke.
One of those moments where you decided
    to make me the modern equivalent of Job
    for one day only.
Can't say I'm laughing.

Where have you been today, Lord?
Why haven't I been able to see you?
Most days I have some sense of you being there,
    of what you are,
    of what everything's about.
But today,

it all just seemed so crowded,
so busy,
so complicated,
that you were nowhere.

I must admit at times I couldn't help but think,
   why me?
Why does this have to happen to me?
It didn't seem fair.
I believe in you
   so why should everything go wrong?
Know what I mean?

Looking back now, Lord,
   I can't help but wonder if the only reason I couldn't see you
   is because I wasn't exactly looking.
I spent most of today feeling sorry for myself
   rather than just getting on with it,
   dealing with it,
   living the day properly
   rather than moaning about it.

I know you were there, Lord,
   with me as everything went wrong.
That's what it's all about really.
Being a Christian doesn't mean getting an easy ride –
   the opposite is so often true.
I guess I just need a helping hand
   to keep focused,
   to not let my everyday life

get in the way
and confuse the issue.

Be in my every day, Lord,
no matter what it's like.

Amen.

Job 1:20-22
When Job heard this, he tore his clothes and shaved his head because of his great sorrow. He knelt on the grond, then worshipped God and said:
  'We bring nothing at birth;
  we take nothing with us at death.
  The Lord alone gives and takes.
  Praise the name of the Lord!'

  In spite of everything, Job did not sin or accuse God of doing wrong.

Job 10:1-2
I am sick of life! And from my deep despair,
I complain to you, my God.
Don't just condemn me! Point out my sin.

Reading the Bible

My main problem with reading the Bible is that I approach it in the same way I approached the books I used to revise from for Biology A level. They were big textbooks full of huge words that meant nothing to me but I had to learn them to pass the test. They were full of descriptions I just didn't understand, solutions to problems I didn't know existed. They were a barrier I had to get over and that was all there was to it. So, too, the Bible. I sit down with it, don't quite know where to begin. I open it, gaze at it and get all confused. I read some of it, don't understand what it's about and feel like a failure. Not the right approach really.

The Bible is a confusing book, but it's also rather amazing. The trick for me has been moving away from seeing it as this huge textbook designed to confuse and fox me and instead approaching it like I would a good novel. Take today. Outside, it's lovely and sunny. I can think of nothing better than sitting out in the sun and reading a book. Why not two books and make one of them the Bible? Why not just start with the basics, get into the Gospels, and just read a couple of chapters, trying to imagine what was actually going on behind the words, what the world smelt like, what the people looked like, how they dressed. Their smiles and laughter, their discussions and arguments. It's then that the Bible comes alive and if things are going really well, I sometimes learn something new about God, about myself and my life, about the world. Amazing stuff.

Lord,
    I did it!
I read the Bible!
Well done me!
I make it sound like it's the first time I've ever done it.
That's not strictly true.
I actually read it rather a lot.
I can't say there's any real plan to how I go about it,
    but I do read it.
I just haven't read it for some time
    and figured I'd let you know
    that I'd just started again.

It was that bit, Lord,
    where the Pharisees bring you a woman
    caught in the act of adultery.
You know, the bit where you kneel and write in the sand,
    then turn and say,
    'OK, if one of you has never sinned, he can throw the first stone.'

But it's how you deal with the woman
    that gets me every time.
The way you just turn to her and say,
    'And neither do I judge you. Go, and do not sin again.'

Lord,
    this is the most wonderful passage.
I find a lot of the Bible difficult to get anything out of.
It's confusing,
    dry,

odd,
unrelated to what I'm doing,
but then something like this happens
and out of all the confusion
sounds a simple message
as clear as a church bell on a frosty Sunday morning.
It's such a lovely passage, Lord,
one where I really can picture what's happening.
It seems so real,
so vivid,
so simple.
What I love, Lord,
is the way you just talk to this woman,
listen to her,
know what's going on
and say, 'I don't judge you either.'

Sometimes,
I find so many people, so many Christians,
desperate to judge others.
There seems to be a tremendous amount
of pointing out the speck in someone else's eye
before dealing with the whopping great plank in your own,
know what I mean?

But here, in this passage,
the words speak for themselves,
simple and effective.
And then you say, 'Don't sin again.'
And why do I find this so amazing?

Because there's no conditions put on this.
You don't say, 'Don't sin again
   and if you do you're condemned for eternity.'
You don't say, 'Don't sin again or it's over,
   you've lost all your chances of getting to heaven.'
No, you just say, 'Don't sin again.'
Sometimes, Lord,
   I find myself so desperate to find a deeper message
   that I miss the pure simplicity of what you were and are about.
This passage,
   your words,
   the whole beautiful incident,
   has opened my eyes again
   to the purity of what you're asking from us
   and showing us.

A picture drawn in the sand so long ago
   and yet so relevant now.

Amen.

John 8:9-11
The people left one by one, beginning with the oldest. Finally, Jesus and the woman were there alone.

Jesus stood up and asked her, 'Where is everyone? Isn't there anyone left to accuse you?'

'No sir,' the woman answered.

Then Jesus told her, 'I am not going to accuse you either. You may go now, but don't sin any more.'

Communion

I love Communion. I always have. The sense of peace, the sense of wonder. The opportunity to simply meditate on an amazing moment in history, on what's happened since, on the implications of everything. It's quite a feeling and never ceases to amaze me. And it's so wrapped up in what Sunday is all about. A time of rest, of quiet. A time to just relax a little, think about what's going on, take stock of life.

But Communion is more than that. It's about real communication, real meaning, a sense of depth to life. It's about refocusing yourself and what you're about, looking at where you're at with your life and God and perhaps readjusting your aim a little.

And then there's the moment when Jesus sat down with his friends and shared an evening and some bread and wine, trying to teach them something that perhaps even today we find difficult to grasp. I know I still do, which is why, when I kneel and take the bread and wine, my mind fills with wonder and a sense of peace that I always try to keep central to what I'm about. It doesn't always work, but it's something to keep aiming for – real communion with God and with each other.

This week, Lord,
   I've experienced two types of Communion.
The first was the usual affair.
A really peaceful service,
   a few wonderful hymns,
   and then just meditating through what Communion
   was all about,
   finally kneeling at the altar,

taking the bread and the wine,
and simply existing in your presence.

It was amazing, Lord,
but sometimes, it isn't.
Sometimes I just go through the motions.
Life's complications crowd my mind
and I go to church,
come home again and am none the wiser.

But then there are times when it all clicks into place.
Where the words sink in and the music drifts through me,
and the whole act of taking Communion
brings me close to you.
I thank you for it, Lord.

Then there was the other communion.
Some friends came round to the house a night or so ago.
We sat round the table,
pulled out a bottle of wine,
some bread, some cheese,
and just chatted the night away.

Now Lord,
I'm not comparing one with the other,
but what I am doing is trying to make a comparison.
At church, through the bread and wine,
I was drawn close to you
as you no doubt intended all those years ago.
That's what it's about really,
focusing on you through the act of Communion
and getting a deeper understanding of it all.

At home,
  through the wine and bread (and that wonderful cheese . . .)
  I was drawn closer to my friends and to what they're about,
  what their life is about,
  where we all fit together in the world.
Laughter filled the air as frequently as we spoke.
Conversation flowed as sweetly as the wine.
It was a communion of friends, Lord,
  and in many ways as vital to me and my life
  as was the Communion on Sunday.

I thank you, Lord,
  for being able to take part in Communion.
There's something about it,
  something I can't quite put my finger on,
  that makes it so special.
And in the same breath
  I thank you for the communion of friends.

Be the bread and wine of my life, Lord.

Amen.

Matthew 26:26-28
During the meal Jesus took some bread in his hands. He blessed the bread and broke it. Then he gave it to his disciples and said, 'Take this and eat it. This is my body.'

Jesus picked up a cup of wine and gave thanks to God. He then gave it to his disciples and said, 'Take this and drink it. This is my blood, and with it God makes his agreement with you. It will be poured out, so that many people will have their sins forgiven.'

Christmas

Come mid-November I don't want to go out anymore. Neither do I want to watch TV or do anything that puts me in touch with people desperate to persuade me that the true meaning of Christmas is getting what you want, or that the true spirit of Christmas can be bought for about 15 quid at 40 per cent proof. The truth about Christmas is still in someone's attic somewhere with a bunch of very old and dilapidated decorations.

I love Charles Dickens' *A Christmas Carol*. It's probably the only film I'm really interested in seeing at Christmas (except *Star Wars*). It's not that I'm really all that interested in what the message of the film is about or what the ghosts are saying to Scrooge. What I am interested in though is the Christmas meal at Bob Cratchet's house. In that scene we have a particularly poor family. One of them is a cripple. The food they have is meagre, but compared to their everyday fare, it's a feast. And they sit around an old table, celebrating who they are and thanking God for what they've got. And, with a little persuasion, they even thank God for Mr Scrooge. It's a beautiful scene, with a simple message, whichever version you end up watching (*The Muppet's Christmas Carol* is particularly excellent). So get a hold of a copy or just read the book and see perhaps a hint of the true meaning of Christmas – thanking God.

Lord,
    it's that time of year again.
Up goes the tree,
    the tinsel,

the rubbish advent calendar.
In every shop window
    appear annoying snow-clad scenes
    involving elves and a fat bloke in a red suit
    (a suit that, if anyone bothered to find out, is actually
    supposed to be green).
Television is instantly given over
    to dedicating all air-time
    to persuading children to annoy their parents
    to buy them things they don't really need.
And everywhere people are spending money they don't have
    on a quick route to dreadful indigestion.

I sound cynical, don't I, Lord?
Like I'm not taking it seriously?
Maybe I'm not,
    and to be honest that really doesn't bother me.
Why?
Well, Christmas is actually rather rubbish.
Or perhaps a more accurate way of putting it is that
    Christmas is actually full of rather a lot of rubbish.
None of what I see around me has anything to do
    with what Christmas is about.
People are celebrating what exactly?
Getting presents?
Getting fat?
Getting great films on TV
    that they've probably seen already?
Doesn't sound worth celebrating to me.
Odd that.

Seems the real reason for celebration
    has been lost,
    thrown out with all the left-over turkey
    no one could really face again.
It's a bit like a cracker in some ways.
Everyone wants to hear the bang –
    it's the very reason for the cracker being there –
    but once done it's forgotten all too quickly
    and everyone's more interested in the presents
    and silly hats
    and rubbish jokes.
I know it's not the best metaphor, Lord,
    but I'm not in the best of moods
    and I think you probably understand.

What annoys me even more
    is that I get caught up in it all.
I find myself wanting things I just don't need.
I suddenly start thinking about all that extra food I need to get
    because without it, it just wouldn't be Christmas.
I buy TV magazines and plan my day of TV-watching –
    like that's such a great way to celebrate
    and so different to any other day . . .

This year, Lord,
    I want Christmas to be as special as it's meant to be.
I want to think about what it really means
    to me,
    to my friends and family,
    to the people I see every day,

to the world.
I want to have a deeper understanding
of how and why you came to us as a child
all those years ago.
I want to smell the straw in the stable,
feel the breath of the animals on my skin,
experience the cold in the air,
understand what it must have been like
not to have been allowed in the house
and instead left in the yard.
That's the Christmas I want to keep in my mind,
to live and breathe through me.

Lord,
meet me in the stable.

Amen.

Luke 2:6-7
And while they were there, she gave birth to her firstborn son. She dressed him in baby clothes and laid him on a bed of hay, because there was no room for them in the inn.

Easter

I remember one particular sunrise service in the Dales. On top of Penn Hill about 20 of us gathered, wondering if we'd ever glimpse the sun again. It was just after six and blowing a gale. We'd all arrived in Land Rovers because that morning they were the only vehicles that would have made it. And as we sang to the morning we stood up to our knees in drifting snow, desperately trying not to lose our place on the service sheet that grew wet and heavy with the snow. It was an amazing morning followed almost traditionally by heading back to church for breakfast. And what a breakfast! Enough cornflakes and cold milk to fill a lorry, more boiled eggs than you could imagine it was humanly possible to boil, wagon-loads of toast and marmalade and hot tea by the gallon. Our faces were rosy, our feet cold and we were with friends celebrating Easter.

In that moment, even if you aren't quite sure about everything that had happened, even if you're beyond confused, there in that moment, something makes sense. There's a sense of hope and a sense of wonder, which is exactly what Easter is all about.

Lord,
    when it comes to Easter
    I still find the whole thing so hard to grasp.
There seem to be so many ways
    of looking at what happened,
    what it's all about,
    why you died,
    why you rose from the grave.

Then there's all the doubt,
    the reasons given for it not being possible,
    that what's recorded to have happened
    never did,
    that it was a lie.

It's confusing, Lord,
    like so much of life,
    so much of faith.
And here I am in the middle of it,
    confused.
No surprise there then, eh?

But to me,
    when I experience Easter,
    think what it's about,
    I'm struck by a simple message.
You died,
    you allowed the world to kill you,
    and in that moment,
    you forgave.
Amazing, Lord.
No amount of praying can add anything to that act.

Then,
    to top it all,
    out of death you came,
    as if to say,
    'Look, don't be afraid!
    Death doesn't win – I'm proof of that. Follow me.'

I know IIiere are plenty of deep theological positions
   on the meaning of your death and resurrection
   but here and now
   to this lowly believer
   sitting on his own talking to you,
   this is what it means –
   to forgive, no matter what,
   and not ti be afraid.

Such a lesson learned, Lord.

Amen.

Luke 23:34
Jesus said, 'Father, forgive these people! They don't know what they are doing.'

Luke 23:32, 39-43
Two criminals were led out to be put to death with Jesus.
   One of the criminals hanging there also insulted Jesus by say-ing, 'Aren't you the Messiah? Save yourself and save us!'
   But the other criminal told the first one off, 'Don't you fear God? Aren't you getting the same punishment as this man? We got what was coming to us, but he didn't do anything wrong. Then he said to Jesus, 'Remember me when you come into power!'
   Jesus replied, 'I promise that today you will be with me in paradise.'

Church

Church isn't about denomination. It isn't about the building or the resources or the number of missions you manage to scrape through in a year. It isn't about doing the best drama production for Easter, having the best nativity scene or the shiniest cross. Church is about the people, not just those who meet together to worship God, but those outside those big wooden doors, the people of the world.

It's simple stuff but we're all guilty of forgetting now and again. We get wrapped up in the big stuff and forget about the little stuff, the things that really matter.

How's this for a challenge – I bet there are people who go to your church whom you don't know. I would even go so far as to say that you may not even know the names of some of them. Imagine a family where you don't know each other. Doesn't make sense, does it? Now, no one says you have to be the best of friends, but why not go over after a service or a meeting and actually introduce yourself? Make a joke about it. Say you can't believe that in a church that's meant to be a family you've never really met before. Have a laugh, a chat. It's easy. Now think about all those outside the church you don't know. All those in need of a helping hand or just a smile now and again. Take the family outside.

That's it, Lord,
    I'm not going again.
I can't bear it anymore.
It's rubbish.
I don't enjoy it,

I don't get anything out of it,
there's hardly any chance to put something into it,
and I'm beginning to lose sight
of the whole point of going.

Yes, Lord,
   I'm annoyed.
Actually no, I'm angry.
I now fully understand why you got so angry
   at the religious types
   when you trod this earth.

It seems that Church has become
   a place for people to spout on about their theories,
   their ideas,
   the things they think we should do.
Some people are particularly vocal,
   almost as though going to church
   is all about us listening to them.

I don't know, Lord.
I guess I just feel
   that we seem to have lost our way a bit.
I've always had this image in my head
   of Church being a community centre.
It isn't a place just for worship involving hymns
   and choruses and sermons and really bad drama.
Neither is it a place just for Christian workshops
   and events involving professional Christians
   helping us become more like them.

(Just a minute, Lord . . .
    need to get rid of my cynical tone . . .)

The Church is a place for the people.
It is a building for the community.
Your Church isn't walls and a steeple
    and fancy tapestries.
Your Church is the street outside,
    the families whom we never see,
    the people hurting,
    the world aching for something more.

In this small place where we are, Lord,
    this Church could be so much more.
People see it as a place where, on a Sunday,
    people wear posh clothes,
    sing
    and then go home – that's it.
It's wrong.
It should be a beacon of hope.
A place always open, always providing.
Somewhere where they know they can go,
    meet people,
    get help and be supported,
    and through it all, learn something of you.
I'm not talking Bible-bashing,
    but showing you through what we do,
    through how we live.
That's what the Church is about!
And here's me spouting off at you,
    getting annoyed

rather than doing something about it.
Leaving won't solve anything
   and shouting at you simply proves
   that I should get on with it
   rather than not.

Your Church is huge, Lord.
We forget that.
We enclose it because it makes us feel safe,
   and you never called us to safety, Lord.
You called us to follow you,
   into the streets,
   into the world,
   into the lives of people who need help,
   need you.

That's the Church I want to belong to, Lord.
The Church that I think, with your help, we could all become.

Amen.

Luke 13:18-21
Jesus said, 'What is God's kingdom like? What can I compare it with? It is like what happens when someone plants a mustard seed in a garden. The seed grows as big as a tree, and birds nest in its branches.

Then Jesus said, 'What can I compare God's kingom with? It is like what happens when a woman mixes yeast into three batches of flour. Finally, all the dough rises.'

Getting it wrong

Hands up, who likes door-to-door salesmen? OK . . . now, is there anyone who really appreciates being pushed into buying anything at all? What about being forced to believe something? Being shouted down and told they're wrong? Having their own ideas and questions ignored?

Jesus called us to pass on what he said all those years ago. He had a message, a fantastic one about eternal life, living a life with God, having a purpose and loving one another – and he wants us to let the world know about it. It's worth remembering though that this didn't come with a set of monthly targets. At no point was there set down an individual evangelism plan. It wasn't a case of, 'the more you bring into the fold, the better your chances of getting into heaven'. No, it was simply, 'Go tell them about it! It's fantastic stuff!'

It's easy to confuse the issue and start pushing people to talk about their beliefs, to come to church to buy the whole package. But look at Jesus for a minute, someone who lead by example. He simply told stories, helped people, showed God's love through everything that he did. Jesus didn't call us to sell the message he brought to us. He called us to love the message and if we do, then we can't help but chat about it now and again, live in some small way like him, let him shine through us. That's getting it right. That's real evangelism.

Sometimes, Lord,
    I get big-headed.
I think I know it all,

that I've got the answers,
that I totally understand.
I stand up and shout people down.
I make other people's ideas sound daft.
I know best, and that's all there is to it.

It's amazing how wrong I can be.
Well, it isn't,
    but I can't really believe I do it so often.

I don't really know why I get like that, Lord.
I guess I just get carried away
    and it's a bit of a security thing, really.
The thought of not being right is so scary
    that it's easier and more satisfying
    to make sure that someone else is wrong.
I come out unscathed.
Well done me.
Or not.

It's not exactly the most Christian way of behaving,
    is it, Lord?
You didn't exactly go around trying to sound great
    and make sure people knew you were most definitely
    and without a doubt
    completely right.
You just sort of joined in the lives of everyone around you,
    the people you met.
You talked with them,
    discussed with them.

OK, so some people felt the sharper edge of your words,
    but you weren't out and about to sound off
    and have everyone 'coo' at your every word
    and say to each other, 'Oh, we're wrong and he's definitely right.'
You simply said what you had to say and let people
    make their own decisions.

Sometimes,
    I really am a fool, Lord.
I forget that what I'm supposed to be doing
    is trying to be like you,
    let you shine through who I am each day of my life.
I'm certainly not meant to be shouting people down.

Help me follow your example a little more closely, Lord.

Amen.

Matthew 4:19
Jesus said to them, 'Come with me! I will teach you how to bring in people instead of fish.'

Ups and downs of faith

I'm as guilty as anyone else. I sometimes think that because I'm a Christian, things really shouldn't go wrong for me any more. It's as if I think I should somehow be protected from life's dangers, as though believing in God gives you a bubble to live in, off which will bounce all the nasty bits of life. The trouble with a protective bubble is that that's exactly what it is, and it doesn't exactly discriminate against what it protects you from. OK, so you'd be protected from the bad, but what about the good stuff? So much of the really great stuff in life has with it that element of risk, of danger. Take these away and there's no challenge to being alive at all. And where do you draw the line? If you're protected against danger, what about failure? No one likes to experience that. But isn't the sweet taste of success partly to do with the fact that you've tried other things and failed? That you've kept going through adversity? That you've never given up no matter how many times you've been tripped up?

Get a note pad or switch on your computer and write down all the successes in your life, all the things that you've managed to achieve, small or big. When you've finished (not that you ever will) look at the list and check out each item carefully, thinking about what it took to make that achievement, the work you had to put in, the risk, what the risks were, what would've happened if it had gone wrong, the number of things that did go wrong until you finally managed to achieve what you were aiming for. Life and faith are stuffed full with ups and downs. But Jesus didn't come here to give us loads of one and protect us completely from the other – that's not what love's about. That's not what life's about. He came to live with us through our lives, through our experiences good and bad. Now that's love. Real love. Eternal.

Lord,
    when it comes to the ups
    and the downs
    I reckon I experience much more of one
    than the other.
I always seem to have something to complain about,
    some reason to be down.
I can always find something I'm not happy about,
    something I wish had gone differently,
    something I wish I'd done better.
Very rarely do I seem to be able to skip and jump
    and yell and scream and shout and cry
    about something that's made me happy.

Faith is very tricky, Lord.
It's such a part of my life
    that it seems to have become knitted into every part of me
    and what I do.
I can't do anything
    without looking for you in it,
    searching for your guidance.
And if something goes wrong?
Well, you're the first one I blame.

If things go wrong,
    how can there be a God?
If my life's rubbish,
    you obviously don't love me
    or I'm just a rubbish Christian.
See what I mean, Lord?
It's a bit of a vicious circle, really.

It's not very clever, I know that,
  and I'm sorry,
  but sometimes it's all I can think to do,
  probably because I'm not really thinking at all.

Am I unusual in this, Lord?
Am I different to everyone else?
Does that really matter?
No, of course it doesn't.
What matters is that I'm being honest
  and admitting that what I do
  isn't really all that clever,
  or helpful,
  or constructive.

Faith, Lord,
  has ups and downs,
  just like life.
And when the two become one,
  nothing really changes that.
The ups still happen
  and the downs are always just round the corner.
But having faith,
  having some reason to live,
  some reason to keep going,
  gives my life more meaning than it would have without it.
Through the ups and the downs
  I'm always looking for you,
  searching for your purpose in me,
  trying to find out what it's all about.

I look up into the stars at night
    and I dream of what's going on out there,
    of the potential of the universe,
    of what it must be like to travel through space.
When I look at my life
    I do the same.
I dream of what's happening,
    what my potential is,
    what will happen as I travel through my life,
    through its ups and downs.

And it's there I ask you to be with me, my Lord.
Through the ups that make my soul scream in joy
    and through the downs that cause it to fall and crawl
    through the mud.
In it all, I ask you to be with me.

Through the ups and the downs,
    feel the tight grip of my hand on yours, Lord.

Amen.

Psalm 23:1, 4
You, Lord, are my shepherd. I will never be in need.
I may walk through valleys as dark as death, but I won't be afraid.
You are with me, and your shepherd's rod makes me feel safe.

Proof

Does God exist? Is God real? Is there a God? What proof is there? How can there be a God with so much going wrong with the world? How can God love us if innocent people are allowed to die? How can God love me if there's so much wrong with me?

Questions, questions, questions . . . Our minds are bursting with them. We can't escape them, we can't ignore them, and most of the time we can't answer them. Especially when it comes to the 'proof' question. Everyone doubts and everyone wants proof. I know I do. I want to see God in front of me. I want to meet an angel. I want Jesus to walk into my room and hold me so tight that I can feel the air squeezed momentarily from my lungs. I want to meet Jesus on a cold winter's day and see his breath in the air. I want to sit by a lake a have him next to me talking about life, sharing some barbecued fish and a bottle of wine. That's the kind of proof I want.

But what proof do I get? In the minds of many, perhaps none. Because to many the love of another person isn't proof of God. The tears of a friend sharing your pain doesn't prove anything. Walking through a woodland, smelling the afternoon air as it runs riot around you has no hint of creativity in it. But that's the proof I've been given and occasionally, just occasionally, it smacks me so hard round the face that tears of pain mix with tears of happiness and laughter and I can't get rid of the smile on my face as, in a moment of madness, all I want to do is climb a tree, paddle in a brook, roll down a hill . . .

Lord,
    I want proof.
I want to feel the closeness of your breath,

the touch of your hand.
I want to see you,
   to hear your voice,
   listen to you.
I want to see your footprints
   and walk with you down a beach.

I want to sit with you one evening
   and talk about my life.
I want to offer you a glass of wine
   and ask you about the meaning of everything.
I want my ears to hear you
   tell me about the universe
   and its purpose.

I want to hear your favourite joke,
   and laugh so much at the punch line
   we both cry and can hardly breathe.
I want to hear about your friends,
   about your time on this earth,
   and how you loved them.

I want you to show me how to fish,
   sit with me in the boat and enjoy my first catch.
I want to see you carve something from wood,
   like Joseph taught you to.
And I want to hear about what you did as a child,
   about the mischief you got into,
   the games you played,
   the friends you had,

what frightened you,
what excited you,
what the world was to you through eyes so young
and yet, perhaps, already so old.

I want to feel you hold me
    as my tears wet your clothes.
I want to know you're there in the darkness
    never leaving my side.
I want to know you so personally,
    so deeply,
    that you become more than just a Saviour
    but a friend,
    a companion,
    someone who understands everything about me,
    who laughs with me and cries with me,
    who hopes and yearns and dreams with me.

Lord,
    I don't want proof,
    I just want you.

Amen.

John 20:27
*He greeted his disciples and said to Thomas, 'Put your finger here
and look at my hands! Put your hand into my side. Stop doubting
and have faith!'*

LIFE

To be old and wise

I have two brothers who, through their erratic, insane, mad, amazing lives, have taught me many things about my own ultimately unusual existence. John, the middle one out of the three of us, disappeared to Australia for a year a while ago. While his mates left university to become career-mad fools, John decided a sheep ranch suited him that little bit better. Twelve months later he arrived back in this country. He'd spent most days out on the ranch, riding motorbikes, crashing cars, shearing dead sheep, experiencing the delights of Australian bars . . . and he looked healthier than a Greek athlete. There wasn't an ounce of fat on him, he was as fit as a really fit thing, tanned, and refused to stop grinning. He'd left this country wondering what life was about and arrived back bringing it with him.

Back at home, as we all sat around in the front room looking through pictures of his exploits and adventures, gasping at the videos of bungee jumps and parachute plunges and laughing at stories about 'who's got the loudest truck' competitions, John decided to bless us all with presents. He handed me a couple of T-shirts and said, 'I figured these would suit you, Dave.' On one were the words, 'Up a mountain, down a beer', which is a rather good motto if you ask me. The other though, has stuck with me since.

I've always been an advocate of doing daft things. After all, with only one life, I'm not really too keen on getting to the end of it and thinking, 'Oh, if only I'd . . .' There's a certain amount of risk in thinking like that, but then without risk I doubt very much that the joy of actually achieving something would be as acute. This attitude has caused me on the one hand to have my long hair permed just to annoy my mum and, on the other hand, jump out of a plane. But the thing is, I regret neither.

Life is an amazing thing. Each and every day I find myself feeling rather amazed about what life is. Sometimes this is mixed with a sense of being rather annoyed or depressed because I look at what I'm doing and feel that I'm wasting precious, God-given time. It's at times like this that I feel as though I've begun to live my life in relative safety, that the risk's diminished a bit and I'm just coasting along from one day to the next. And then I think of this T-shirt. In that room with my more-alive-than-life-itself brother and the rest of the family, I read the words, 'To be old and wise, you must first of all be young and stupid'. He grinned at me and I grinned back; an acknowledgement that at last we'd found a motto for the way we three brothers seemed to live our lives. OK, so Jesus didn't actually say, 'Be a bit daft – it's great!' And neither will you find this approach to gaining wisdom in the Ten Commandments (bit of a shame if you ask me . . .). Yet in it, there is some sense of what God wants us to do with our lives. Wisdom doesn't come with age and youth doesn't walk hand-in-hand with stupidity. Yet wisdom, risk and life are all connected – take away one and the other two fade. If we want to make something of our lives, actually totally live, then risk and a bit of stupidity and the courage to really take our lives and live them to the full are what we need to do. And to do all this in the presence of God – now that is life.

Matthew 19:29-30
All who have given up home . . . or land for me will be given a hundred times as much. They will also have eternal life. But many who are now first will be last, and many who are last will be first.

I feel so alive

You may not like the music but there's a band called P.O.D. (Payable On Death – I'll let you figure out what they're on about . . .) One song on their album, *Satellite* is called 'Alive'. I urge you now to find this song wherever you can and drench yourself in the lyrics. I want you to learn them and commit them to heart. Get a hold of the song and you'll know why.

Jesus came to give us life so that we could live it to the full. What does that mean to you? What does living it to the full really do to you as you sit reading this? Are there things you would like to do but thought you were perhaps a bit old? Is your life a bit nine to five? Are you missing out on what real life feels like? Do you remember what it feels like?

I jumped out of a plane once. I don't think I've ever felt so close to death in my life. But the flip side of the coin? I've never felt so alive. I want to feel like that every day I'm here. I want to be so alive that when my time is finally up I'm not too bothered because I'm exhausted, tired and can look at a life stuffed full with life. I want to be able to look Jesus in the eye and say, 'See? I lived! I really did! Yes, I've done a lot of things wrong, but I lived, Lord! I took my life as the gift you intended and really lived it!' I want to squeeze the juice from my life until there's nothing left, and keep on squeezing. Live life to the full. Be able to say to yourself, 'I feel so alive!'

Lord,
    this is one of those rare moments
    where I have the urge

to just run headlong down this hill in front of me
and dive into that lake at the bottom.
The sun's shining,
    the air's sweet.
I can hear creation singing its song.
And me?
Well, Lord,
    today I feel so alive.

If today were a song I'd be a huge drum solo,
    crashing and banging and thumping.
Or a guitar screaming its soul to the sky.
If today were a painting
    I'd fill it with so much colour.

I've never felt so alive.
No reason really,
    just one of those days where you wake up,
    breathe in,
    and for just a moment,
    just for that time,
    everything comes together and makes sense.
A smile slices your face into a picture of joy,
    your body buzzes
    and when you go outside
    all you want to do is run around
    like a young version of yourself in a huge country park.

I want to climb trees
    and roll down hills

and swing on ropes hanging from branches over rivers.
I want to do cartwheels really badly,
   ride my bike so fast my lungs hurt
   and throw freshly cut grass high in the air.

Today I'm so alive
   I could burst.
Today I'm so alive
   I wish I were a bird so that I could fly free,
   soaring high and diving at breakneck speed.

It's on days like this, Lord,
   that I can sense you running with me,
   joining in the joy that life gives,
   smiling at the happiness it brings.

Today, Lord, I feel so alive
   and I thank you for it . . .

. . . and I'll race you to that tree . . .

Amen.

John 10:10
I came so that everyone would have life, and have it fully.

Career

I've never been very good with the whole career concept. I blame my parents. Not because they never gave me any guidance. The exact opposite in fact. I wasn't brought up believing that life is about scoring a top job with a top firm, that achieving something has everything to do with a pay rise. Instead, I was shown that life is much, much more. It's about doing something you believe in, making something of yourself, having something to show for what you've done, doing something worthwhile that you love.

That's not the kind of answer careers advisers want when they ask, 'So, what do you want to do with your life?' They really don't know what to do at all if you turn round and say, 'I want to do something that means something, that has an impact, that makes my life a life worth living.' You can imagine the look on their face when I said, 'I want to be a writer.'

Life has its responsibilities. There are certain things you generally have to do if you want to live and one of these is pretty much about getting a career. But a career isn't the be-all and end-all of what life's about. There's much more to it than that. Bills have to be paid, food has to be bought, but perhaps occasionally we all need to just stop and think about where our lives are going and think to ourselves, 'Is this the right way to go?'

Lord,
   I don't want a career.
I don't want to have to think about
   promotion
   or getting paid

or pensions because all it seems to do
is get in the way of life.
Does that make sense?

I know I have to work through my life
but the last thing I want is to spend the weeks of my life
simply carrying out a job
to earn money
to keep me alive
until I retire,
look back at it all,
and feel amazingly unimpressed.

When it comes to careers, Lord,
so many people seem to settle on one of two things.
It's either all about the money
or it's a case of what else can I do?
I can't do either of those, Lord.
Well, for a start, it can hardly be all about the money
when you look at what I'm doing.
And if it's a case of what else can I do, then if this is it
take me now, stop my life,
because it's a waste.

I have other ideas, Lord,
other ambitions.
I know what I really want to do with my life.
There's risk involved
and I know lots of people probably think I'm mad.
Some things will have to sacrificed,
scary decisions will have to be made,

but that's what I want, isn't it?
I don't want the safety,
    I don't want the security.
After all, I don't remember hearing anything
    in your words to us
    about getting nice and secure.
I think the opposite was the case.

Lord,
    I know there needs to be balance,
    that I can't just jack everything in
    and run for this horizon dream I'm so desperate to achieve.
I need to be sure about the steps I'm taking,
    think about the risks involved
    and make sure I'm not being foolhardy
    (not that I would ever be that, Lord).

Getting a balance in life
    between what you need to do
    and what you want to do
    is a real challenge, Lord.
With the safety
    comes the risk,
    with the exciting
    comes the mundane,
    but through it all
    I can see some sense of where I'm headed.

Help me keep sight of that horizon, Lord.

Amen.

Matthew 16:24-28

Then Jesus said to his disciples, 'If any of you want to be my followers, you must forget about yourself. You must take up your cross and follow me. If you want to save your life, you will destroy it. But if you give up your life for me, you will find it. What will you gain, if you own the whole world but destroy yourself? What would you give to get back your soul?

'The Son of Man will soon come in the glory of his Father and with his angels to reward all people for what they have done.

'I promise that some of those standing here will not die before they see the Son of Man coming with his kingdom.'

Tomorrow

Two prayers about one thing in a book? Why? Easy – it's something that is not just a priority but also something we think about pretty much every day of our lives. There's not a day goes by without us thinking about what comes next, what could happen if, what might happen, what tomorrow could bring. So here's a challenge. For the rest of the day when you find yourself thinking or worrying about tomorrow, try to make it a positive moment rather than a negative one. Try to get excited about what tomorrow might bring rather than being frightened about it. Turn worries into anticipation, excitement, wonder. Isn't that what tomorrow should really be about if we're going to think about it at all?

Lord,
    what's tomorrow all about?
It's scary to think
    that I don't know what will happen in it.
OK, so I've got some idea,
    but so much is left to chance.
There are so many variables,
    so much that can't be planned for.
When I think of it like that
    it's hard to believe I make it through any day at all
    and survive to see the next one.

I know it's exciting, Lord,
    but the scary stuff sometimes takes over
    and the mind dwells on the worst

of what could be
    rather than the best.
Some people call this being realistic.
Me, I just think that it's a waste of today.

I know some of what tomorrow will hold
    and I know some of tomorrow
    holds stuff I could never know about
    until it happens.
That's what makes life so rich,
    so huge,
    so amazing,
    and so very, very short.

Worrying about tomorrow
    isn't going to help me
    when it happens,
    be it the tomorrow
    happening after today
    or the tomorrow
    happening in years to come.

Tomorrow is perhaps nothing more
    and nothing less
    than a corner in a road,
    a bend in the path,
    the brow of a hill.
You don't know what you'll see
    till you get there,
    you don't know what you'll discover,

what you'll find,
what you'll experience.

I thank you for tomorrow, Lord.
See you round the corner.

Amen.

Luke 12:22-30

Jesus said to his disciples, 'Do not worry about your life! Don't worry about having something to eat or wear. Life is more than food or clothing. Look at the crows! They don't plant or harvest, and they don't have storehouses or barns. But God takes care of them. You are much more important than any birds. Can worry make you live longer? If you don't have power over small things, why worry about everything else?

'Look how the wild flowers grow! They don't work hard to make their clothes. But I tell you that Solomon with all his wealth wasn't as well clothed as one of these flowers. God gives such beauty to everything that grows in the fields, even though it is here today and thrown into a fire tomorrow. Won't he do even more for you? You have such little faith!

'Don't keep worrying about having something to eat or drink. Only people who don't know God are always worrying about such things. Your Father knows what you need. But put God's work first, and these things will be yours as well.'

Death

I will die. It's a reality. I can't change it. One day all that I am will stop. I find it impossible to believe that when it happens that's it, end of story. On the other hand I sometimes find it impossible to believe that there is anything more. Then I think of Jesus. A person in history. Someone real. He wasn't some made-up individual, a fictional character, he was real. Someone who walked and talked and laughed and cried. Someone who had friends, family. Someone who saw the same sun as me rise into the sky and then set in the evening. A real person who said lots of amazing things that I try to put into practice in my life. A real person who died and, according to the Bible, rose from the dead and ascended into heaven. It's at this point my brain freezes and doesn't know what to do. I know there are the stories and ideas that this didn't happen, that the body was stolen, that the disciples made it up. Then I think about the disciples and how human they were, how scared. What would they have done if Jesus hadn't risen from the dead? Would they really have gone around saying that he had, that he was the Christ? Would those fishermen, those personal friends of Jesus, spread the word and die for it and watch others die for it? The whole thing is one massive paradox. And then I think, if Jesus, this person who walked this earth, did rise from the dead, did see his friends and tell them not to be afraid and that he'd meet them in paradise . . . is he not saying the same thing to me? To all of us?

Lord,
    I went to a funeral a couple of weeks ago.
The sun was out,
    the church was packed.

Smiles and tears and silence
    filled the air.
It was a peaceful event,
    a day of sadness
    but also of thanks.
I was proud to have known
    the person who we'd all lost.

Now,
    looking back on that day,
    the thought of death scares me a little,
    or in truth,
    a lot.

I remember looking at the coffin,
    thinking about what was left of the person I knew so well.
It didn't seem real.
I could still hear her voice in my head,
    the jokes she would tell,
    the stories.
I could still feel what it was like to kiss her goodbye,
    to walk with her,
    to sit and just chat.
Nothing I could do could make me think she
    was gone for ever.
It just didn't make sense.
But where is she now, Lord?
No trace of her remains,
    just memories.
Is she with you?

I believe this to be so,
　but when faced with the stark reality of death
　it's hard to believe completely,
　no matter how much I want to.

I know, Lord,
　that one day what is left of me
　will lie in a coffin.
People who know me
　will be at that funeral,
　singing songs I've chosen,
　but I will not be there,
　just my shell.

I pray, Lord,
　that on that day
　I will be with you
　in your kingdom
　and will know no fear of death
　and fully understand
　how and why
　you took away its sting.

Amen.

1 Corinthians 15:54-55
The bodies we now have are weak and can die. But they will be changed into bodies that are eternal. Then the Scriptures will come true, 'Death has lost the battle! Where is its victory? Where is its sting?'

Pressure release

Pressure is as much a part of life as eating and sleeping. At work, at home, down the gym, on holiday, it seems to follow us like a rather annoying and very faithful dog. There are times when you feel so run off your feet that you don't know how to stop. Other times it seems that the easiest thing to do would be to explode. And then there are those moments when all you want to do is punch the wall until your knuckles bleed.

We all seem to forget that like a pressure cooker we need a release valve. There's no point just letting it build and build until the lid flies off. It's very messy and takes ages to clean up. Instead we need to manage the pressure in our lives, deal with it, and give ourselves ways to release it. Easier said than done, especially when we're all so good at excuses; the best of all being, 'I simply don't have time'. Trouble is, if this is the case, we're time-bombs just waiting for some inappropriate moment to explode.

If we live lives full of pressure and nothing else we soon end up no use to ourselves, to others, to God. If that's not enough incentive to relax then I don't know what is.

Lord,
 I've just got back from the gym,
 and this shower is both necessary
 and enjoyable.

I'm exhausted, Lord.
My muscles ache

and I'm still a little out of breath.
I really pushed myself tonight,
   lifted more,
   ran further,
   sweated.
It felt great.

My body may be hurting, Lord,
   but my brain feels so much clearer.
Work was a nightmare today.
Too much to do
   in not enough time
   for lots of people
   who all insisted
   their jobs
   were the most important
   on my list.
By the end of the day
   I felt fit to burst.
I could feel the pressure
   building up in me.
Kept clenching my hands
   on my way home –
   never a good sign.

At the gym
   I focused totally on what I was doing.
All the pressure of the day,
   all the pent-up aggression
   that comes from a day

of annoyance
was channelled into each exercise.
And as the sweat ran
   so the pressure released.

Now, Lord,
   under this shower,
   I feel calmer,
   more relaxed.
The pressure of the day has eased,
   my brain doesn't feel so cross-wired,
   and now all I want to do
   is stand for a few minutes,
   drenched in hot water,
   listening to you.

Amen.

Numbers 6:24-26
I pray that the Lord will bless and protect you, and that he will show you mercy and kindness. May the Lord be good to you and give you peace.

My body

Wherever you go, whatever you're doing, image is thrust at you. You can't hide from it or run from it. The world seems utterly convinced that the only thing to do is to convince you to buy this or do that to look like this or smell like that. And it's gone beyond make-up and hairstyles and the clothes you wear. Now we've got the body perfect to achieve. Every man must have a six-pack and biceps like knots in ships' rope. Every woman must have a flat stomach, no cellulite and a bottom so firm it could knock down walls.

I'll be the first to admit I'm not happy with the way I look. I've a bit of flab I want to get rid of and I'm not the toned person I was when I was 18. But at the same time I'm not living the same life. How I look has a lot to do with how I live and sitting behind a desk for seven hours a day doesn't lend itself to a Herculean physique! If it did, I'm sure my job would be very oversubscribed indeed . . .

It's all about perspective. I may never achieve the body I really would like, but do I really need to? What's important is that I stay as healthy as I can and as healthy as I want to. This body is a gift and the only one I'll ever have so I'd better look after it. But that doesn't mean getting obsessed. My weakness isn't that I love to eat enormous amounts, just that I like good food and enjoy cooking it. I like tastes, food that inspires and gets you excited. I'm a foody and on the other hand someone who'd like to look a little better than he does. I've a feeling God wants me to enjoy both and too much of something always leads to imbalance. I eat too much, I get fat. I get obsessed with how my body looks, I don't get to enjoy food. Strike a balance though, and I'm some way to getting where I want to be. And through it all the most important thing is remembering never ever to neglect what's on the inside . . .

I'm getting older, Lord,
and my body doesn't look too impressed.
Doesn't seem long
since I was able to eat anything I wanted
and stay slim.
Now I can certainly pinch more than an inch,
and I'm not happy about it.

It's not that I'm vain, Lord,
just worried that this body you gave me
is beginning to look a bit run down.
It's the only one I've got
and I don't really fancy it turning into an old banger
quite yet.

It's hard to work out what to do.
Actually, it isn't –
it's just hard to work out how to do it,
how to make the time.
The solution is quite simple really.
A sensible diet, some serious exercise
and in a few months I'd have a decent shape back,
rather than one which I disguise with loose-fitting clothes.

But how do I find the time?
How do I find the energy?
My body is the visual evidence
that my life isn't in balance,
that my priorities are wrong.
There's no excuse to look like this,

no matter how stressed
or overworked.

I need to make time, Lord.
I need to get up half an hour earlier each morning
    and go for a walk or a bike ride.
I need to walk to town
    rather than drive.
And as for eating?
Well, it doesn't really take much to sort it out,
    does it?

Lord,
    I look at myself and realise
    that although I've become busy elsewhere in my life
    I've become very lazy when it comes to looking after myself.
And lazy is a horrible word, Lord,
    one which my dad drilled into me as a child
    as one of the bad things in life that you shouldn't become.
But then that comes from a man
    who has never stayed in bed after 6am,
    who's worked the early hours
    to sort things out for the day ahead
    and who yet still has time for you . . .
Amazing, Lord.

So,
    as I cover myself up,
    hide away what I've become,
    help me look at my reflection

and realise I can change the way I look.
Not through pride or vanity
  but through necessity
  and respect
  for this gift you have given me.

See you down the gym, Lord.

Amen.

Genesis 1:26-28
God said, 'Now we will make humans, and they will be like us. We will let them rule the fish, the birds, and all other living creatures.'

So God created humans to be like himself; he made men and women. God gave them his blessing and said: 'Have a lot of children! Fill the earth with people and bring it under your control. Rule over the fish in the sea, the birds in the sky, and every animal on the earth.'

Ambitions

Ambition is a dangerous thing. It changes the way you look at your life, changes the direction it's going in. It changes the things you do, how you spend your time, how you spend your money. It changes your priorities, takes your time, uses all your energy. It also shapes who you are, what you want to be, what you will become.

Like anything, ambition can take over, but it doesn't need to. The solution is keeping God at the centre of it all. Ambition is a part of life, not the aim of it. What you want to be or do or achieve isn't all your life, just a bit of it. An important bit, but not something for which everything else must be sacrificed. Real ambition doesn't cause other things to fall by the wayside. It doesn't change who you are. Real ambition is something people can see in you and understand rather than resent or be afraid of. Real ambition has God at its centre. After all, achieving something is one thing, but achieving it with God? Well, you decide . . .

Lord,
    you know me so well.
You know everything that I am,
    everything that I may well become.
Even my ambitions.

My ambitions are big, Lord,
    always have been and always will be.
My parents always said I was a dreamer
    as a child.
As I grew older,

the dreams became ambitions.
And ambitions are awkward things,
    because they don't fit in with the way the world
    wants you to live your life.
And I like that.

Ambitions can make it impossible to conform.
You can't be like everyone else if you want to catch
    exactly what the ambition is all about.
You've got to live differently,
    have different ideas,
    different aims,
    different priorities.

It's hard for some people to understand.
They see it as foolish,
    not thinking about what it's like in the real world.
But in the real world my dreams, my ambitions,
    are still possibilities.
They're certainly not things I packed away with my toys
    as I grew older.
I kept them with me,
    shaped them,
    moulded them,
    and they're as much a part of me
    as my arms or my brain.
Without them I wouldn't be who I am,
    to me, to my family, to my friends.
Everyone knows me not just as a person
    but also by my ambitions.
Take them away,

stop going for them
and I'd no longer be who I am,
who you created me to be.

Sometimes, Lord,
    I do wish I could just forget about them,
    get on with what everyone else seems to think is important.
It seems attractive and certainly safer.
But I can't,
    I just can't do it.
I can't deny who I am.

In these ambitions, Lord,
    I venture to think that occasionally,
    just occasionally,
    I see a glimpse of your handiwork in them,
    as though the seeds of these dreams were planted long ago.

They're still growing, Lord –
    help me to keep feeding them.

Amen.

Colossians 1:10-12
Then you will live a life that honours the Lord, and you will always praise him by doing good deeds. You will come to know God even better. His glorious power will make you patient and strong enough to endure anything, and you will be truly happy.

    I pray that you will be grateful to God for letting you have part in what he has promised his people in the kingdom of light.

Mates

One of the richest things in life is friendship. I count myself as one of the luckiest people on earth when I look at the friends I have. I could have everything I own stripped away from me, but I'd still have my friends – people I depend on and people who know they can depend on me. The people I've grown up with. And when I look at Jesus I feel right at home. Why? Simple – he too surrounded himself with friends. These weren't people he figured needed his help and direction and that was it. These were people he loved and trusted. People he sat down and ate and drank with. They shared his life, his ups and downs. They talked together, walked together, laughed and prayed together. They were friends, real friends. And if Jesus needed that close group of friends how much more do we need those around us? And how often do we really truly let them know what they mean to us and how valuable they are?

Lord,
    this is a thank-you.
I know most days
    I just seem to turn up and have problems
    to bother you with,
    but this time it's different.
I want to say thanks for my mates.

The friends I've got now, Lord,
    are quite simply amazing.
We've known each other for years,

been through a lot,
from college, through marriage and beyond.
There are jokes and running gags
that we still tell
though we've forgotten how they originally started.
There are stories we still tell again and again
because it's great to relive old times
with such big smiles on our faces.

And we're only at the beginning of our friendships, Lord.
We've the rest of our lives to grow through together
and that's so exciting.
To think that we'll see each other grow old,
develop,
achieve.
To think as well that we'll be there for each other
through the tougher times of life,
whatever they may be.

Friendship, Lord,
seems to me to be the most valuable thing around.
You could take away everything I owned
but so long as I still had my friends,
I reckon I could survive quite well.

For them, Lord,
I give thanks.

Amen.

1 Samuel 20:42
Jonathan said, 'Take care of yourself. And remember, we have each asked the Lord to watch and make sure that we and our descendants keep our promise for ever.'

Job 2:11
Eliphaz from Teman, Bildad from Shuah, and Zophar from Naamah were three of Job's friends, and they heard about his troubles. So they agreed to visit Job and comfort him.

Job 6:14
My friends, I am desperate and you should help me, even if I no longer respect God All-Powerful.'

On the train

Something about train journeys has always fascinated me. Car journeys are cool, but a train? That's something else. It's you, a bag of kit, a book or two, some music, and a destination. You're on your way from one place to another and all you can do is pretty much just let it happen.

On a train, you're almost free. You can sit there and forget about where you've come from, where you're going to and just get on with gazing out the window and dreaming of. . . well, whatever you want to dream of. Mountains and lakes and high waterfalls, the sensation of white sand hot under your feet, time with friends, seeing somewhere you've never been before.

Train journeys also give you that sense of anonymity. A chance to be a face in a crowd, alone to the world. It's just you, the world whizzing by and just next to you, all around you, is your Creator listening to your thoughts.

Lord,
    I'm on a train.
The world's whizzing by at some crazy rate
    and I'm surrounded by people I don't know.
I've been sitting on the floor for the past two hours
    and have only just managed to get a seat to myself,
    it's that busy.
And somewhere on this train
    I've put my suitcase . . .
    I just can't quite remember where.

I love being on a train, Lord.
I've got everything I need with me
   (which isn't much, as we both know)
   and I'm off travelling somewhere.
Even though I know where I'm going
   there's a tremendous sense of freedom
   about getting on a train,
   a sense of freedom that sometimes
   I think is missing from my life.

It's not that I want to escape, Lord,
   just that life has this way of tying you down,
   restricting you,
   keeping you penned in.
I don't think it's really meant to be like that, is it?
The idea that life is here to trap us,
   restrict us?
Mind you,
   looking at the way many of us live our lives
   you'd think that was certainly the case.

When I get a taste of freedom
   it's something so fresh,
   so vibrant
   that I want more.
Free from just living day to day,
   just to get to the next week,
   that's freedom.
It's not anarchy
   or ignoring your responsibilities.

It's about taking responsibility for your life
   and having the freedom to make something of it,
   not to be afraid of what that freedom might bring.

On this train,
   I know the freedom I'm experiencing is only short-lived,
   that I'll soon be back at my desk
   typing my way to another completed 9 to 5.
I don't want to forget this moment though, Lord.
As trees smudge themselves behind this window
   into a world of greens and browns and blues,
   I don't want to forget that my life
   needs freedom to become what it's got the potential to become,
   the freedom to breathe.

Help me stay free, Lord.

Amen.

Psalm 119:45
I have gained perfect freedom by following your teachings.

2 Corinthians 3:17
The Lord and the Spirit are one and the same, and the Lord's Spirit sets us free.

Rainy days

Rain can do two things – take you up or take you down. Bring life or just make it seem even worse. It's hard to beat running through a heavy downpour which takes you by surprise on a hot muggy day. The flip side is when you're feeling down and it starts to rain. The rain comes on and everything just gets a whole lot worse. It's bleak outside and inside. It's as if the world's reflecting exactly how you feel.

The temptation on a day like that is to lock yourself away, sit inside and feel sorry for yourself. Next time it happens though, try something different. Grab a Bible and read your favourite bit, the one bit you can almost remember the verses of, the bit that inspires you, sums everything up. As soon as you've finished it grab a coat and get out into the rain taking the words you've just read with you. Now walk in the rain, get your hair wet, feel the drops sting your face, water running off your fingertips, your shoes and legs soaked. Breathe in the world, the smell of the water, remembering the Bible verse. Think about what else is going on in the world, what lies beyond this day and how you feel and, if you can, stretch out your mind and catch a glimpse of what you believe in.

It's raining, Lord.
Again.
We were blessed
    with a brief glimpse of sunshine
    and now this.
Dreary, cold,
    dark rain.
Wish I'd stayed in bed.

There are times, I know,
   when I love the rain.
When it's the best thing on earth
   to walk out into it,
   to get drenched,
   soaked to the skin,
   to feel it sting your face,
   run into your mouth,
   forcing you to close your eyes.
That kind of rain breathes new life into you,
   gives you a sense of being a part of the whole world.

But there are times when the rain is like this, Lord,
   and I don't like it.
I'm allergic to weather like this.
It just makes me grumpy.
I'm an outside person
   and all this weather's doing
   is forcing me to stay in
   and I don't know what to do with myself.

I could read a book I guess,
   but I'd rather read outside.
I could do some writing,
   but I'd rather do it outside.
I could listen to the radio
   and have a nap . . .
   but I'd rather do it outside.

See the pattern, Lord?

Trouble is, when I get in this mood
   nothing's right
   and everything's wrong.
My tea's either too hot or too cold.
The chair's always too soft or too hard.
I need a good slap.

You know what, Lord,
   I think I need a walk.
It's absolutely appalling outside
   but I don't care.
The fact that I can hardly see the other side of the street
   doesn't matter.
I'm going outside,
   into the storm
   rather than hiding away in here
   and complaining about it.

There's a lesson in this somewhere, isn't there, Lord?

Amen.

Genesis 9:16
When I see the rainbow in the sky, I will always remember the promise that I have made to every living creature.

Matthew 5:45
. . . He makes the sun rise on both good and bad people. And he sends rain for the ones who do right and for the ones who do wrong.

THE WORLD

Just look at it!

I'm a dreadful climber. I make stairs look like the north face of Everest. I climb by throwing myself against rock in the hope that the momentum will help me stick to it. And yet, weekends in the open air with friends are fabulous – being away from the rush and push of my everyday life, sitting out in the open with people who don't mind my company, cooking on a camping stove, lying out under the stars, wrapped in a sleeping bag. On my last climbing trip with my two brothers it was a beautiful sunny day at Stanage in Derbyshire and there was just enough chill in the air to give you a rosy face and make you keep your jacket on. The actual rock face is possibly one of the forgotten wonders of the world, stretching for miles, dotted with climbers trying to scale it. I was sitting at the top of a climb, tied into any amount of anchor points to make sure I was nice and secure. As one of my brothers made their way up the rock, I was struck by the awesome view before me.

From that cliff I could see for miles. The sky was bright and aeroplanes were carving it into parallelograms. The fields were vibrant green and the wind carried the echo of bleating sheep and the occasional chug of a tractor. If I could have bottled how I felt at that moment and sold it, I'd be rich. I was momentarily fortunate enough to experience perhaps a little of what God feels when he looks at his creation. Yes, there's a lot wrong with it. There's war, famine, homelessness, persecution, loneliness, pain, and confusion. But now and again, we need to remind ourselves why we're trying to change all that.

We get hung up on the idea that what's really important is doing God's work and getting to heaven. But is that all there is to it?

Shouldn't we start to think about our responsibility towards this planet we have been so graciously given? Were we really created so that we could spend our years trying to prove our worth and ourselves so that we could get to heaven?

We were created out of pure, unconditional, wildly creative love. We were put on this amazing planet because God so loved the world and us. We are responsible for looking after it, getting involved with it, loving it. Occasionally we need to sit back and stand in awe at what this planet really is, what it's capable of, why it is so extraordinarily amazing.

That day was a take-your-breath-away moment. Believing and following Jesus is about getting involved in this world. We need to get out there, stand under this vast canopy of stars and clouds and sunlight and rain, and have nothing more and nothing less to say to our God than, 'Just look at it!' And then to never ever be able to get rid of that almighty God-given grin etched into our wind-red faces.

Mark 16:15
Then he told them: 'Go and preach the good news to everyone in the world.'

Romans 1:20
God's eternal power and character cannot be seen. But from the beginning of creation, God has shown what these are like by all he has made. That's why those people don't have any excuse.

Genesis 1:31
God looked at what he had done. All of it was very good!

Jesus in every face

Pick a morning and go for a walk into town. This time though, try to look at it through new eyes. Try to see something new, something you've never seen before. Explore shops and cafés you've never ventured into. And while you're doing all this, check out the people around you, the ones pushing past you or trying to sell something to you. Look at them, picture everything they could be. Try to guess what they do, what's happening in their lives, where they're going.

One thing I find amazing is that every life is completely original. If I go out into town this very minute I will brush past people who have their own dreams, worries, fears, loves, hates, futures, pasts, hopes, ambitions, friends. People who, like me, are trying to live their lives to the best of their abilities, to get something out of it. Now that adds up to one huge amount of life going on in just the town where I live. What about this country? The world? And then I think about what Jesus thinks of each and every person, the potential he sees, the love he has for them. At moments like that, I am in awe. I may never fully understand everything about what goes on in the world or about what the Christian faith is, but that sense of wonder about what this world is and what it's capable of . . . I will always be amazed.

Lord,
    you got a minute?
Just come back from a trip into town
    and fancied a chat.
Just a minute, the kettle's boiling . . .

. . . right, Lord, you see the thing is,
I was thinking
about something I once heard someone say.
It went something along the lines of
    trying to see Jesus in every face.
And this morning, it was rather difficult.

From grumpy people in queues
    to screaming children and their even louder parents.
From teenagers doing their teenage thing
    to twenty-somethings trying to look wealthier
    than they actually were or would ever be.
Everywhere I turned, everywhere I looked,
    I couldn't see you at all.

Am I blind, Lord?
Am I supposed to be able to go out
    and just see you everywhere?
Ah . . . I see . . .
    I'm missing the point.
Can't say I'm surprised really.
Walking around town didn't put me in the best of moods.

Perhaps then it's more about seeing the potential
    of everyone if they knew you.
Does that make more sense?
Seems to, to me anyway.
I don't know if that thought scares me
    or excites me really.
Trying to come to terms with the potential you see in everyone
    is too much for my tiny brain,

but I can see where you're coming from
and also where I fit in.

Sometimes, Lord,
when I'm out and about
I know that if someone were to look at me
they probably wouldn't see your face shining back at them.
They'd see anger or disdain or contempt or . . .
well, a whole bunch of stuff
that doesn't have much to do with you.
And if people aren't seeing you through me,
someone who follows you,
where does that leave us?

Help me, Lord,
to see you in everyone else
and everyone else to see you
in me.

Amen.

Matthew 5:13-15

You are like salt for everyone on earth. But if salt no longer tastes like salt, how can it make food salty? All it is good for is to be thrown out and walked on. You are like light for the whole world. A city built on top of a hill cannot be hidden, and no one would light a lamp and put it under a clay pot. A lamp is placed on a lampstand, where it can give light to everyone in the house. Make your light shine, so that others will see the good that you do and will praise your Father in heaven.

Blue sky

Journeys can seem to go on for ever, can't they? In the car, traffic jam after traffic jam, you need to stop, think about where you're going, why you're taking the journey and refuel both the vehicle and yourself. You need to pause, rest, take a breather.

Life races on and if we're not careful, days turn to weeks turn to months turn to years. Before we know it we've got older and not appreciated getting there. Rest is vital. It gives us a chance to look out beyond the confines of what we're doing as an individual and take a glance at how amazing being alive just really is. Do yourself a favour. Stop. Sit. Look out. Appreciate. Pray.

Lord,
    what can I say?
What words can I possibly find
    to express how I feel right now?
There aren't any,
    but I have no choice.
Faced with what I'm looking at this moment,
    I just have to speak,
    I have to voice something,
    anything,
    to let you know.

Before me, Lord,
    sweeps a valley.
The blue sky, speckled with dusty clouds

holds a sun whose warmth
is cooled by the faint breeze
sweeping through the air.
If I close my eyes
I feel almost as though I'm flying,
stretching out my hands to embrace the day,
letting my head fall back
to take almighty gulps of the scent of the moment.

I'm standing stunned by your creation.
I could pray about how we're destroying it,
how we're ruining what you have given us,
but this is not the moment for that, Lord.
This is a moment for praise.
A moment which can only be captured
in the mind of the witness.

Standing here
I feel cleansed,
washed.
There's something in your creation
that, when the moment's right,
stares me right in the eye
and says, 'Everything is OK. See?'
And I smile and know,
that just for that brief moment,
nothing could make me happier.
Nothing.

It is that moment that I'm experiencing here and now,
with you.

It is that moment
   that I'm imprinting on my mind,
   storing in my memory
   almost as a get-out-of-jail-free card,
   so that I will always remember
   there is something more
   to life
   when those times come
   that feel as though life is utterly pointless.

To be born into such a beautiful world,
   to be given the chance to stand here,
   to watch and listen and learn,
   is to know that you are with me
   and that I am a part of whatever it is
   this world is for.

It's wonderful, Lord.
Thank you.

Amen.

Genesis 2:1-2
So the heavens and the earth and everything else were created. By the seventh day God had finished his work, and so he rested.

By the river

There are moments in life you treasure. Moments that your brain locks away in memory under 'special'. They become memories that no matter how you feel can bring a smile to your face, cheer you up, make you laugh. It's these moments we live for.

What amazes me though is how every single one of these moments in my mind was in essence, so simple. They didn't involve vast amounts of money being spent. They didn't involve huge effort and organisation. They were, more often than not, moments with people I love, just enjoying each other's company. Tents in the rain, walks by a river, barbecues in a garden. None of them grand, none of them worthy of a novel, none of them expensive . . . but all of them priceless.

Lord,
    I'm a countryside junkie,
    an addict of fields
    and forests.
I get a high
    from a crisp early morning,
    dew frozen to the grass,
    rooks in the trees.
It's what keeps me going,
    gets me up in the morning,
    helps me survive work,
    feeds my soul.

At the weekend, Lord,
   I went for a walk with a friend.
It was a beautiful Sunday,
   which felt as though the world was resting.
The sky almost clear
   and the air sweet –
   you could almost drink it.
After a quiet mug of tea in a café
   we strolled along a river,
   under the shadow of a castle.

The world felt so alive, Lord,
   and it rubbed off on us.
We were excited to be a part
   of what this world is,
   of what it's about.
We talked about our lives,
   what directions we were heading in,
   what we wanted to do with them.
Our dreams, our aims,
   everything, Lord.

Later on we grabbed some sandwiches
   and sat in some light rain on a bench,
   simply smiling.
It was one of those moments, Lord,
   where you feel as though the world
   is on your side.
It was brief,
   fleeting,
   but it was so real.

Smiles stuck to our faces
  and we couldn't get rid of them.
Everything made sense,
  everything felt right,
  in that moment.

That day, Lord,
  I had no questions,
  no desperations,
  no worries.
Something about your world
  took me,
  held me,
  and told me
  that I was a part of everything going on around me.
That I had purpose
  and had every right to dream
  about where my life was going,
  where you were helping me get to.

Lord,
  meet me by the river.

Amen.

Romans 1:20
God's eternal power and character cannot be seen. But from the beginning of creation God has shown what these are like by all he has made. That's why people don't have any excuse.

Comparisons

Spend the next five minutes comparing yourself to other people. Compare what you have to what they've got. Compare your salary or your house or your car. Compare your holidays and your clothes and your TV. Compare your furniture, your friends, your careers.

Stop.

How do you feel? Pretty dreadful? As though everyone else is doing better than you, has more than you, has a more fulfilling life than you? What have you gained from this exercise? Exactly – nothing at all except an extreme case of envy.

It's almost impossible not to compare yourself to other people. In some respects a bit of healthy competition never hurt anyone. But comparing has nothing to do with envy. There is, after all, only one life, one example, one person you should be comparing yourself to and I doubt he's all that interested in what car you wish you had.

Lord,
  what's going on?
Why do I feel like this?
It's wrong, isn't it?
I know it is,
    I'm sure it is,
    but sometimes
    I can't help it.

If I just switch on the TV
    my answer stares me back in the face.

I complain about where I am,
   what I have or haven't got,
   get envious of other people.

Then I see so many others
   across this globe
   who have so little.
Whose own lives
   make mine look so blessed,
   so rich.

Is it human nature, Lord,
   to be like this?
Sometimes I'm so happy with where I am,
   what I'm doing,
   what I've got,
   that I just grin.
But other times,
   what I haven't got
   and what I haven't done
   eat away at me,
   make me grumpy.

Stupid really, Lord,
   I know that.
It doesn't get me anywhere,
   it doesn't help,
   it doesn't make me achieve anything.
But it creeps up on me,
   takes over.

I think my problem
   is that I confuse what I want my life to mean,
   to achieve,
   with what I want to see as a result of it.
Know what I mean?
I want to be successful in what I do,
   get somewhere,
   but sometimes that translates into material goods,
   being well known,
   and on really silly days,
   being famous.

Your world though, Lord,
   has a way of snapping me out of it.
Whether I'm walking or driving
   or just sitting around,
   it reminds me of what I have got,
   where I am going
   and how lucky I am.

Lord,
   I don't want these thoughts to cloud my mind
   of what's really important.
My life has already been blessed in so many ways
   and when I look back at where I've come from
   and when I sometimes get a little peek
   at what's round the corner
   I can see your hand in it.
I want to stay focused on you,
   not lose sight,

accept what I've got,
and be happy with it
and go from there.

The only comparison I should be making, Lord,
is my life with yours.

Amen.

2 Corinthians 12:9-10
'My kindness is all you need. My power is strongest when you are weak.' So if Christ keeps giving me his power, I will gladly boast about how weak I am. Yes, I am glad to be weak or insulted or ill-treated or to have troubles and sufferings, if it is for Christ. Because when I am weak, I am strong.

Another bomb

I don't have an introduction to this. I only have this prayer and many, many more. Words fail . . .

I can't believe it, Lord,
   I just can't.
It seems impossible
   that this still goes on,
   that people think this is the way
   to make things right.
Another bus, Lord,
   another person strapped up with explosives.
Apparently the blast was so huge
   the bus was thrown several feet into the air.

I don't have words, Lord.
I don't understand why these things happen,
   I don't understand why innocent people die,
   why other people kill them,
   why revenge breeds revenge.
It's senseless to me,
   sitting so far away from it all
   and all I can do is weep.

I sometimes wonder if I'd feel any different
   if I were in the thick of it,
   right there,

knowing what was going on,
breathing the smoke and the fumes of death.
What would I think then?
Would I see why they did it?
Why people had to die?
Why children, the old and the young,
　　men and women,
　　were disintegrated in a second
　　because someone had a point to make?

Even faced with that situation,
　　I still don't know.
It's as though the people of this world
　　are desperate to pull it apart,
　　to shatter it,
　　scream it apart at the seams.

I can do nothing, Lord.
I'm here and I'm helpless
　　as another revenge attack
　　leads to another suicide attack
　　leads to more retribution,
　　more revenge,
　　more death.
My words and my thoughts
　　seem empty.
All I am left with is you.
All I am left with
　　is the hope
　　that there is hope in this world

that one day,
whenever it may be,
everyone will look back at the history of the world
and know they have learned a very great
and very painful lesson
and never,
ever
forget the deepest of scars.

Amen.

Acts 7:27
But the man who started the fight pushed Moses aside and asked,
'Who made you our ruler and judge?'

Will we make it?

Buy a newspaper or watch the news. Count up the number of articles or reports which have something good to say about what's going on in the world. Do the same for those stories which aren't all that positive. Rather out of balance, isn't it? Try and keep a file for a week of good and bad news stories, just to re-emphasise the point.

The trouble with news is that if it's good, no one wants to report it. There's no drama, no conflict. Which leaves the rest of us with the impression that everything in the world is going wrong. So, is it? Is this world really bent on self-destruction? Are we doing all we can to mess things up? Or is there hope? Is there a chance that we can sort it out, work together and turn this planet into God's vision for where it should be?

Lord,
    will we make it?
Will this race of beings
    created in your image
    end up where only you know
    they can get to?
Or will we blow it,
    ourselves,
    the world,
    into oblivion?

It's a tough one this, Lord.
I look at the world and see so much potential,

so much ability,
so much creativity.
And at the same time I see so much hate,
so much pain,
so much destruction.

I often wonder what it would be like
if the whole world
worked together.
If we could all just agree
on some basic human rights,
realise we're together,
celebrate rather than annihilate our differences,
what then would we be capable of?
The possibilities are endless,
exciting,
terrifying,
amazing.
You must want to just walk away at times, Lord.

I sit in awe of what this world is,
how dynamic,
how diverse,
how beautiful.
Sometimes I almost cry
realising that in my short life
there are huge areas of it
I'll never see.
Is that daft, Lord?
I don't think so.

Makes total sense to me.
I love this world,
   this planet floating in space.
It's so impossible,
   so completely incredible,
   that all I can do is gasp.

Lord,
   I pray for the world.
Its people,
   its creatures,
   its total creation.
I pray that everything
   will one day come together,
   that it'll all make sense,
   that differences will be lost,
   old disagreements forgotten
   and that tomorrow really will be
   as great as you know
   it can be.

Amen.

Matthew 5:3, 18
God blesses those people who depend only on him. They belong to the kingdom of heaven!

Heaven and earth may disappear. But I promise you that not even a full stop or comma will ever disappear from the Law. Everything written in it must happen.

Money

Nothing I own has much to do with making me happy. That's not me being self-righteous, it's just a fact. Which is why I get annoyed when I find money getting in the way. I need money to live, to pay bills, buy food, get to work. That's fair enough, but when I start thinking to myself that I need more stuff, better things, that I don't have enough money to live a worthwhile and satisfying life, that's when I start getting frustrated. Money has a nasty way of wriggling its way into places it has no right to be.

Jesus had plenty of little chats with people who had problems with money. So why not go back to one you probably haven't read much since Sunday school. That lovely story of Jesus meeting with Zacchaeus. Read it, learn from it, then read it again. Sometimes, Jesus' actions and words are so simple that their message is even stronger.

Right,
    that's it, Lord.
Take it all away
    and let me live a life
    where I don't need it,
    any of it.
Where I don't have to spend my life trying to get it
    so that I can spend the rest of it
    getting rid of it
    or swapping it for stuff
    that 90 per cent of the time
    I don't actually need.

Money, Lord,
  it's getting on my nerves.

As I'm getting older, Lord,
  I'm beginning to realise how many people my age
  have done so much better than me already
  (I am talking in monetary terms here, Lord).
I don't know how it's possible.
It's not like I haven't tried.
But now I find myself experiencing pangs of envy.
I try to stop it,
  but I can't help but want that car just ahead of me
  and I bet the house it's driving back to
  is so much nicer than mine.

There, Lord,
  I've admitted it:
  I do experience envy,
  I do covet what my neighbour has;
  which is why I'm talking to you about it,
  because it's driving me nuts.

I don't want for anything really, Lord.
I have plenty,
  have enough to live a life I utterly love.
But that doesn't stop these feelings.
The world's way gets at you now and again,
  and you find yourself sliding into that need
  to always get more,
  have more,

buy more,
need more.

I know that I'm at my happiest
　when I have the least.
Be it on a train,
　cruising somewhere in a car,
　living out of a rucksack,
　sitting at the front of a tent.
Then, Lord,
　am I truly happy.

I don't want the gloss
　because what I have is so real,
　so wonderful,
　that I'm happy.
Then the moment ends,
　I'm back in the world of the everyday
　and envy starts to eat away at me again.

Lord,
　I don't know quite what to do about it.
I know it's wrong,
　I know I'm wrong.
I know it only makes me grumpy,
　which is why I'm confessing
　because I need your help
　to help me wake up,
　so that next time I look at what someone else has
　and wish I had the same,

I'll realise I'm not just happy without it,
I'm happier not even thinking about it.

Life isn't for the buying,
   it's for the living – and that's all I'm interested in.

Amen.

Luke 12:16-21

A rich man's farm produced a big crop, and he said to himself, 'What can I do? I don't have a place large enough to store everything.'

Later he said, 'Now I know what I'll do. I'll tear down my barns and build bigger ones, where I can store all my grain and other goods. Then I'll say to myself, "You have stored up enough good things to last for years to come. Live it up! Eat, drink, and enjoy yourself!"'

But God said to him, 'You fool! Tonight you will die. Then who will get what you have stored up?'

This is what happens to people who store up everything for themselves, but are poor in the sight of God.

3000 AD

I love science fiction. Just by looking at some of the awful videos I own, you can see that! I've always been fascinated by the future, by space travel, by the stars. Something about it all always made my imagination run wild. What would space travel be like? What's it like in other star systems? Are there other beings on other planets? I find questions like these so exciting that when, on a clear night, I look into the stars, I can't help but dream of what might be, what will happen if everything goes right with the world.

So perhaps *Star Trek* is a bit far-fetched. Perhaps our imaginations have created things that will never ever be. But the possibility of what might happen is quite astounding. Just consider how much the world has changed in only 100 years, one lifetime. Praying about today is important, but we need to remember the future as well, the people who'll live it and work through it and explore it. Tomorrow's people will see and do things we can only imagine. It's an amazing thought, isn't it?

Lord,
    I'm staring at the stars.
You know,
    I'd love to travel into space,
    explore it,
    find out what it's really like out there,
    what's actually going on
    behind the little lights
    and the scientific equations
    which seem to hold them in their place.

Are there other worlds?
Are there other creations?
Somewhere, is someone or something
   looking up
   and asking the same questions as me?

I wonder, Lord,
   what it'll be like in a thousand years' time.
I have this insane hope and trust
   that this world has every chance of making it
   there and beyond.
That with this kind of potential
   it simply can't be wasted.
Will we travel to the stars?
Will light speed become a possible impossibility?
Will we colonise other planets,
   treat spaceships and space travel
   like cars
   and a trip to the supermarket?

I can't hide from the fact
   that I secretly hope this is the case.
Neither can I hide the fact
   that I envy the future
   and the people who'll experience it.
It's so exciting to think about what could happen.
I know so much could go wrong,
   but perhaps we need to start dwelling on the possibilities
   rather than the obstacles?

I don't know, Lord.
All I do know is that as I gaze heavenward,
  as I look to the stars,
  I pray for tomorrow's people
  and for the lives they will lead
  as we race to the stars
  and beyond.

Amen.

Ephesians 4:10
This also means that the one who went deep into the earth is the same one who went into the highest heaven, so that he would fill the whole universe.

Hebrews 11:3
Because of our faith, we know that the world was made at God's command. We also know that what can be seen was made out of what cannot be seen.

Arms wide open

A sense of helplessness can all too easily take over when we look at what's happening to the world. From the destruction of the rain-forests to homelessness, there seems to be just so much pain. When it all becomes too much, when we don't even have the words, it's hard to see how we can do anything to stop what's happening. As if our lives, no matter what we do with them, will have no effect.

But when I think like this, I remember that one man. He must have been grubby and sweaty from work. His hands would have been callused and hard from the wood and his muscles strong from bringing in the wood to work with. This was a man who knew what a hard life of work meant. Who had a trade, who worked with other people in a town no one really cared about. That man got up, said things, did things, suffered for it, and made a difference. A difference so amazing that 2000 years on we're still recoiling from the shock. Who says one person can't make a difference?

Lord,
    at times
    this world takes me
    and forces me to stand
    and despair.
It stares me in the face,
    challenges me to do anything else
    but weep for everything going wrong.
I feel helpless,
    tired of the pain that seems to seep

from every crack
in every pavement
in every part
of the world.

It looks at me,
    silently screaming.
No words,
    just a sense of agony,
    as though words would make the pain
    less real.

What use am I to this,
    I think to myself.
How can I help?
How can I do anything
    when faced with so much gone wrong?
I'm just one person,
    one soul.

There's no answer, Lord,
    that I can see.
Sometimes
    I join in the pain
    and cry with the world,
    hoping at least
    that by some small miracle
    my sharing of the pain
    will ease it slightly.

Then other times
   I can do nothing
   and sit motionless
   in front of the TV,
   in bed,
   at work,
   in a café.
Stunned to silence.

What use can my life be
   to this seemingly endless destruction
   of something so valuable?
What use can I make of what I am,
   what I'm capable of?
I have skills,
   I can use them,
   but will they have an effect?
Will I just be wasting my time?

'Follow me,' you said.
You lead by example.
If anything, your life shows us
   that it is possible to make a difference.
I know that because 2000 years on
   I'm sitting here
   searching for your guidance.

Lord,
   I stand with my arms wide open,
   naked to the world and everything in it.

I want to hold it,
  help it,
  weep with it,
  heal it.
I may be just one person,
  that may be all that I have,
  but it's also everything I'm going to give.

Amen.

Luke 23:33-34, 46-47
When the soldiers came to the place called 'The Skull', they nailed Jesus to a cross. They also nailed the two criminals to crosses, one on each side of Jesus. Jesus said, 'Father, forgive these people! They don't know what they are doing.'

Jesus shouted, 'Father, I put myself in your hands!' Then he died.

When the Roman Officer saw what had happened, he praised God and said, 'Jesus must really have been a good man!'

Looking out the window

Stop what you're doing and go to a window. Look out of it. Try to search for something you've never seen before. Look further, wider, deeper. Really strain to see exactly what's in front of you, no matter what it is.

That world outside our window is all we've got. That's it, end of story. Either we look after it and each other, or we blow it. It's easy to hide away in our own little lives. Easy to just keep our heads down and get on with what our lives are about, where our lives are going, what our lives mean to us. But we need to think big rather than small. We need to look out of our windows rather than just shutting the curtains. And then we need to go further. We need to open our doors and walk out into that world and get involved. We need to experience it and love it and nurture it and care for it. Only then will the view beyond our windows become something so amazing that ignoring what we see would be an impossibility.

Lord,
    I want to celebrate something.
I want to look beyond the obvious,
    see past the dirty
    and praise you,
    shout your name,
    yell out loud
    about this world.

Everywhere I go
    things seem desperate to tell me
    how awful this world is.

I can't hide from its pain.
I can't run from the things that are going wrong.
And, Lord,
    if I were to believe the hype,
    I'd give up now,
    drop out,
    pack it all in.

The only news you ever hear is bad news.
Wars here,
    famine there,
    hatred here,
    desperation there.
This is a world falling apart,
    pulling itself to pieces.

In some ways, Lord,
    I can't deny it.
I can't see all the problems in the world
    and ignore them
    or pretend they'll go away.
But what I can do
    is look beyond that.
Probably a bit like what you do
    when you look at us.

There is something inherently wonderful
    about this world, Lord.
It's an amazing place
    jam-packed with variety,

    surprises,
    adventure,
    danger,
    colour,
    life.

Lord,
    how can I look out of my window
    and deny such wonder?
I can't!
I just can't do it!

Take me for example, Lord.
You must look at me
    and see so much dirt,
    so much that you don't want to be there.
But you look beyond that.
You see my potential,
    my capabilities,
    what I could become,
    the beauty of what I'm really like
    when I'm with you,
    when you're in my life.

I can't help but look at the world
    and do the same.
There's so much dirt on the window
    but beyond that,
    so much scenery
    that it takes my breath away.
I don't want to spend my life

concentrating on the smudges,
the grime.
There's no hope that way.
But there is hope in what's beyond that,
what's beyond the glass.

There's a world, Lord,
with so much beauty,
so much soul,
that all I can do
is kneel
and thank you –
and pray
that one day
everything will come full circle,
and the dirt will fade,
the pain disappear
and your world will shine like the jewel in the cosmos
you always knew it could become.

As I look out the window, Lord,
help me see the beauty beyond
rather than always concentrating
on the dirt on the surface.

Amen.

Romans 8:18-21
I am sure that what we are suffering now cannot compare with the glory that will be shown to us. In fact, all creation is eagerly waiting

for God to show who his children are. Meanwhile, creation is confused, but not because it wants to be confused. God made it this way in the hope that creation would be set free from decay and would share in the glorious freedom of his children.

John 3:16

God loved the people of this world so much that he gave his only Son, so that everyone who has faith in him will have eternal life and never really die.